Flicking Your Creative Switch

Q: How many publishers does it take to screw in a light bulb?

A: Three. One to screw it in. Two to hold down the author.

Flicking Your
Creative Switch

Developing Brighter Ideas for Business

Wayne Lotherington

John Wiley & Sons (Asia) Pte Ltd

Copyright © 2003 by John Wiley & Sons (Asia) Pte Ltd
Published in 2003 by John Wiley & Sons (Asia) Pte Ltd
2 Clementi Loop, #02-01, Singapore 129809

Other Wiley Editorial Offices

John Wiley & Sons, Inc., 111 River Street, Hoboken, NJ 07030, USA
John Wiley & Sons Ltd, The Atrium, Southern Gate, Chichester PO19 8SQ, England
John Wiley & Sons (Canada) Ltd, 22 Worcester Road, Rexdale, Ontario M9W 1L1, Canada
John Wiley & Sons Australia Ltd, 33 Park Road (PO Box 1226), Milton, Queensland 4064,
Australia
Wiley-VCH, Pappelallee 3, 69469 Weinheim, Germany

Library of Congress Cataloging-in Publication Data:
ISBN: 0470-82103-5

Typeset in 11/16 points, Times Roman by Linographic Services Pte Ltd
Printed in Singapore by Saik Wah Press Pte Ltd
10 9 8 7 6 5 4 3 2 1

To my girls,

Yen, Rachel, Merin and Maxine

Contents

PART II: Kick-start Your Creative Habit

Preface

Welcome to *Flicking Your Creative Switch*. This book is all about creative thinking and how to get ideas to solve your business problems – whether they be small or large.

The tools that you'll find here have been gathered from sources as diverse as the art world, advertising, the music industry and education. In our Creative Thinking workshops we have seen some sensational ideas generated with these tools, some of them coming in a matter of minutes.

It seems everyone has a favourite creative thinking tool. Some find the "Eyes of Experts" a quick and easy way to come at a problem from another point of view. Others like "What's Hot?" for its relevance to today's society. Or "Random Word" to get their mind associations racing. Or the Surrealist technique called "Exquisite Corpse", which is one of my favourites.

But regardless of which tool you like best, let me encourage you to use a variety of the approaches and not to fall back on just one or two methods all the time or your opportunities for creativity will be limited. And of course, you'll improve your ability to use these tools and think creatively the more you use them.

A number of people have helped me with this book and I would like to express my gratitude to them. My wife Yen for her encouragement and patience, my friends and colleagues Bob Irwin, James Glenn, Vivek Kuchibhotla and Simon Kornberg. Plus my daughter Rachel Lotherington for her love and knowledge of surreal art, Rick Woods for giving me the push I needed, and the hundreds of workshop participants who have told me time and time again... *"you should write a book"*.

Well, here it is. I hope you will enjoy *Flicking Your Creative Switch* with me.

Wayne Lotherington
Singapore, 2003

PS Make Creative Thinking a habit.

Foreword

I have known Wayne Lotherington since 1965 when we were both in the same class in high school in Australia. That school did its best to stifle any creativity anyone showed. There were more rules than students and anyone who showed even the slightest difference or independence was soon urged to conform… *or else*. We both had our fair share of "or elses".

And it's not just at school that we're taught to conform. The pressures to conform are all around us because while conformity kills creativity, it also brings order, predictability, harmony and a feeling of security.

But in today's ultra-competitive world, conformity is also the road to boring advertising, me-too products and brand oblivion. Being different is what today is all about. Standing out. Getting noticed. And it's not just true for brands. The same applies to all of us as individuals. Thinking creatively gets us noticed, gets us jobs, wins promotions and it brings financial success. And it makes life more interesting.

Flicking the 'Creative Switch' should be a goal for all of us, whether we're a CEO (Chief Executive Officer) or CSO (Chief Sweeping Officer). We could all be more creative in our jobs – *and often that means more effective* – if we just knew how. The problem is however, that despite all those years at school and in business, most of us live our lives without knowing the very simple secrets of creativity. No one ever taps us on the shoulder and says, "Pssst… want to know how to be creative? Here's all you have to do…"

But that's exactly what Wayne's book does. It contains the secrets of Creative Thinking that many successful people use naturally – without even knowing it. Wayne also shows that creative thinking is about simplicity, and he explains and demonstrates it in an uncomplicated and engaging way.

By reading *Flicking Your Creative Switch* and applying the tools, you have the opportunity to unleash your creative powers. So don't wait any longer, turn the page and start flicking your creative switch.

Allan Pease

January 2003

Number 1 bestselling author of

Body Language and *Why Men Don't Listen &*

Women Can't Read Maps

PART I
Intelligence, Knowledge, Creativity

Q: How many mutants does it take to change a light bulb?

A: Two-thirds.

Intelligence and Creativity are two different things. You can be Intelligent without being particularly Creative. And you can be Creative without being particularly Intelligent.

And Knowledge? We have all met people who are walking encyclopedias, yet some aren't exactly Intelligent or Creative.

Unfortunately most societies focus more on Intelligence and Knowledge than on Creativity. Mothers are told that their child's intelligence starts in the womb so they are careful about what they eat and drink. That breast fed is best fed because it improves brain development. And we've all seen ads for baby food and milk formulas that show babies wearing mortarboards as if they are graduating from university at the age of two. So much effort has gone towards promoting intelligence.

Then Knowledge takes over. Parents buy their five year olds science books to read. They send them off to school where their heads are filled with fact after fact. The children receive private tuition to ensure they know everything required to pass their exams. And we tend to judge a child by his or her school grades.

What about Creativity? No one teaches us how to think more creatively. In other words, in the pursuit of Intelligence and Knowledge we neglect the one thing that might make Intelligence and Knowledge useful.

But gladly, things are changing. The fact that you're reading this book is evidence of that.

In Part I we will define Creativity and see why there has been a recent change in attitude to it. Following that we will learn how we can all be more creative. Then we'll discuss how the creative mind works so that you can make the best use of yours. In Part II we will examine a number of Creative Thinking tools.

Now let's start work on our Creativity.

1
Creativity and Innovation:
The Latest Buzzwords

Q: How many Magicians does it take to change a light bulb?

A: It depends on what you want it changed into.

It seems the whole world is talking about Creativity and Innovation. Those two words are everywhere from the Classroom, to the Boardroom to the Cabinet-room. They have become today's buzzwords, like *paradigm*, *deliverables* and *imperatives* before them.

I remember when, not so long ago, the only people talking about Creativity were in the arts, music, Hollywood or advertising. But now everyone is referring to more creative ways of thinking, of teaching, of expressing ourselves, of presenting, of developing products and services, of dealing with customers, of growing businesses, and of building nations.

Innovation and Creativity are more than just buzzwords. Creativity itself can become a way of life and Innovation the result of that behaviour. We are moving from a service society to an ideas society and Creativity and Innovation aren't just the words of the ideas society. They're the means to it.

The words Creativity and Innovation are often used interchangeably, even though they mean different things. So let's start by getting our heads around Creativity and Innovation: what they are and why everyone is so interested in them.

What is Creativity?

In a Creative Thinking workshop with advertising agency M&C Saatchi Singapore, I asked for a definition of Creativity. The team came back with many good suggestions, but the one we all liked the most was based on the word Creative, spelt backwards. That is, EVITAERC. They decided it stood for "Every Virgin Idea Takes A lot of Energetic Raw Courage".

They went on to explain that Creativity is about getting ideas. That the ideas must be new or fresh. That the ideas are the result of effort. That we need courage to come up with these fresh ideas, because there will be others around us who don't like risks. We all agreed it provided great insight to Creativity and that it did so in a creative way.

Now let's see what the experts say about Creativity.

Edward de Bono says, *"Creativity is a messy and confusing subject and seems to range from devising a new toothpaste cap to Beethoven's writing his Fifth Symphony. Much of the difficulty arises directly from the words 'creative' and 'creativity'."*

He says that creative, at its simplest level, means *"bringing into being something that was not there before"* and contends that by that definition even creating a mess is Creative. Yet, he says, a mess doesn't necessarily add value even though it is new.

From there de Bono points out that creative output shouldn't be easy or obvious and that there should be something *"unique or rare about it"*.

Finally he says that the concepts of unexpectedness and change may give us a different view of Creativity.

So what is de Bono saying? Besides saying Creativity is hard to define, I think he is saying that Creativity is bringing about something that is new; that adds value; that isn't obvious or easy; that is surprising or unexpected.

The Campaign Palace, an Australian advertising agency, defines Creativity like this: *"Creativity is shaping the game you play, not playing the game you find."*

Campaign Palace says that most people and organisations are rarely creative, instead they live their lives and go about their business *"according to established 'rules' or conventions"*.

Campaign Palace believes that *"truly creative people and companies have the imagination to see beyond the present reality and invent new, different and better ways of doing things."*

Dilip Mukerjea, describes creativity as *"the spark that ignites new ideas"*. In his book, "Surfing the Intellect" he provides a formula for creativity. He says the formula is C = (ME)$^\infty$.

$$C=(ME)^\infty$$

In this formula, C = Creativity; M = mass of data, information, knowledge and wisdom acquired over your lifetime; E = the sum of Experiences and the Enlightenment gained thereby, that serve to Energise your life.

In other words, Creativity is the *"infinite capacity that resides within you"*. It involves combining information with your life's experiences.

And finally, Bob Irwin, my friend and one of my business partners expresses it like this: *"Creativity enables people to connect seemingly unconnected things and from that connection, new ideas spring forth."*

Now, let's take all that wisdom from M&C Saatchi, de Bono, the Campaign Palace, Mukerjea and Irwin and get a simple yet useful definition of Creative Thinking and Creativity. It all seems to be about "new" and "ideas". So how about...

Creative Thinking is the behaviour we use when we generate new ideas. And Creativity itself is the merging of ideas which have not been merged before. New ideas are formed by developing current ones within our minds.

Let's see if we can turn that definition into a graphic.

The Light Bulbs

Ever noticed that when a cartoon character gets a new idea, a Light Bulb appears above his head? The Light Bulb has become a metaphor for an idea. In fact, in Spanish, the phrase for "I have an idea" is "se me prendio el bombillo". This literally means "my light bulb went on". So let's see how we can use the Light Bulbs to explain Creativity.

Light Bulb #1:
Something we already know

Light Bulb #3:
The new ideas we develop, based on merging #1 and #2.

Light Bulb #2:
Another thing we already know, but unrelated to the first thing

The roll-on deodorant, invented by George Thomas, is an example of this kind of thinking. His Light Bulb #1 was Deodorant. He already knew about that. Light Bulb #2 was a ball point pen. He knew about that too, but not in the context of deodorant. He combined them to get his idea of a deodorant that could be applied in the same way that a ball point pen applies ink to the paper.

And Betty Nesmith combined two ideas to invent something we all know. Her Light Bulb #1 was a problem: typing mistakes (in the days before computers). Her Light Bulb #2 was something she also knew but didn't associate with typing mistakes: paint. Her idea was to use paint to cover up typing mistakes. And the product? Liquid Paper.

These are just two examples of new ideas being generated by combining two existing ideas. But this explanation of where new ideas come from isn't just restricted to big ideas and new products. The same applies to the small ideas we get everyday. Like in this example:

Let's say that you have been driving to work via the same route for the last five years. You're quite satisfied with your way of getting there. But this morning your partner has asked you to drop off some urgent dry cleaning on the way to work. The trouble is that the dry cleaners is quite a long way off your normal route to work. Nevertheless, you agree to do it.

So you start off from home and make your detour to the dry cleaners. When you get there, you drop off the clothes and get back into the car. Now you have a choice to make. You can either play it safe, back-track and join your usual route to work. Or you can try to find a new way to work from where you are right now. This represents an opportunity to be creative.

Let's say you take the opportunity and, after zig-zagging your way down some unfamiliar streets across town and making some intelligent guesses, arrive at work. You've found a new route. You look at your watch and find you're no later than usual, despite the stop at the dry cleaners. You've actually found a new, efficient way to work. Your creativity paid off.

How does this fit with the Light Bulbs?

Light Bulb #1:
Your tried and tested
5-year route to work

Light Bulb #3:
A new route to
work via the
dry cleaners

Light Bulb #2:
Annoying trip to the
dry cleaners that
forces you from your
normal route

Life is full of Light Bulb #1s: things you already know or just noticed; they are the status quo. Light Bulb #2s are the stimuli that can prompt you to come up with your new idea. And every time you bring them together you can create something new.

Get used to seeing those Light Bulbs in this book – and in your future. We'll use them in our explanation of how ideas are developed as well as in our examples.

Now What is Innovation?

While Creativity is about new ideas, Innovation is about putting the ideas into practice. Of course, you wouldn't put an idea into practice unless you expected it to provide some value. Hence, according to Innovation Network USA, *"Innovation is implementing new ideas that create value."*

Or in the words of Bob Irwin, *"Creativity is a behaviour whereas Innovation is a process that makes ideas useful... when the best idea emerges from the pack and is put into action."*

So innovation is the pay-off when an idea becomes an outcome. You do it by testing ideas, selecting the best ones and implementing them.

For George Thomas the creativity was applying deodorant through a roll-on action. The innovation came about when the idea was turned into a real product. And for Betty Nesmith, the creative idea was using paint to cover up typing mistakes. The innovation was Liquid Paper. For your trip to work, the idea was to find a new route via the dry cleaners and the innovation was the actual route you discovered and will use from now on.

The Link

So the link between Creativity and Innovation? Creativity is finding new ideas. Innovation is the product, service or policy that results from putting the idea into practice.

Between Creativity and Innovation we need one more step:

Evaluation, or validation. Not every idea is worth implementing. We first need to assess an idea's value. Will it work? Is it cost effective? What are the consequences, direct and indirect? The process looks like the chart on the previous page.

Getting back to George and Betty, the Evaluation stage for their ideas would have included market research, manufacturing issues, studies on cost effectiveness, testing, market trials and so on.

For example, just thinking about manufacturing issues for the deodorant:

- How big should the ball and the rim be to let just the right amount of deodorant through?
- How thick should the liquid be?
- What shape should the product be to make it easy to hold and use?
- What sort of cap will keep the deodorant from drying out or leaking?
- How big should the product be?

Liquid Paper would have had its own set of manufacturing issues to resolve. I don't think it was just a matter of filling little bottles with Berger Paint's Luxol Silk Splendour in Whispering White and attaching a brush to the lid.

Now we understand the simple relationship between Creativity, Evaluation and Innovation, let's make it more realistic.

The More Realistic Link

In the real world, Creativity often starts with Need Identification, where ideas are sought to solve problems. This is a case of necessity being the mother of invention. But sometimes people come up with ideas without having a particular brief or problem in mind. Perhaps this is a case of invention being the mother of necessity. In the Creativity stage, ideas are generated without evaluation, because premature evaluation tends to stifle creativity.

Once ideas are generated they are evaluated. This can result in ideas being rejected, accepted or being "sent back" for further development. Once accepted, ideas then move to the Innovation stage, where a prototype, sample or pilot is often used to fine-tune the product or service.

There may be a need for further modification, where something that sounded good in principle doesn't turn out quite so well in reality. "Back to the old drawing board."

Assuming the prototype, sample or pilot survives – with or without modification – the next step is Implementation. In commercial ventures the Implementation stage involves the 4 Ps of Marketing: Product, Pricing, Promotion and Place, leading up to the launch of the innovative product or service.

So it looks like the chart you see on the next page:

Evaluation, Innovation and Implementation are only relevant once you have your creative ideas, so I'm going to leave them up to you and concentrate on Creativity in this book. We'll discuss how all of us are creative, how our minds work and how to *flick our creative switch* in our daily business lives.

Thinking Out of the Box

Creativity is often associated with the phrase "thinking out of the box". The phrase comes from the Gottschaldt figurine, also known as the 9-dot game. The game works like this:

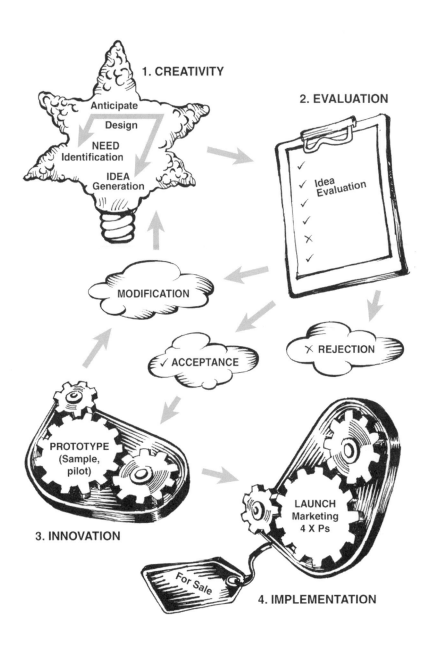

Using no more than 4 straight lines, join all the dots without taking your pen off the paper.

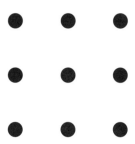

If you think of the dots as a box, as many people do, then you can't solve the problem.

There are several ways to solve the Gottschaldt figurine, but all require thinking outside of the imaginary box. And the box? It represents the restrictions we impose upon ourselves. We will discuss those restrictions and where they come from in Chapter 3. Meanwhile, try solving the figurine. Now that you know it requires thinking out of the box, it shouldn't be too hard. (Two solutions are shown on page 151)

So thinking out of the box is about looking beyond the obvious, trying new ways, not being fenced in, being prepared to venture out and explore, and escaping self-imposed limitations.

Of course the trouble with any word or phrase is that if it is over-used, it eventually becomes a cliché and we lose sight of what it really means. I have met people who use the phrase "thinking out of the box" yet don't understand it. Worse still, I have met some who know what it means but continue to think inside the 9-dots. So here's a little challenge for you...

Put a Lid on the Box

Why follow everyone else and talk about thinking out of the box? Put a lid on it. Be original. Think of a new phrase to remind yourself to think creatively. And only use it while it helps you. When it loses its sting, make up another one.

We sometimes do this little exercise in our workshops and we've had some very interesting results. A few of the words and phrases that have come up are "boxless thinking", "disobviate", "originizate", "dotty thinking" and "stretchy brain". My own phrase for Creative Thinking is *"Flick the Switch"*. It's what I tell myself when I want to be more creative. It doesn't matter what word or phrase you choose or whether it means anything to anyone else, so long as it prompts you to think more creatively.

So what's your word or phrase going to be?

Thought Starters

You can use these exercises to check your understanding of Chapter 1 and to start thinking about your own job and the need for Creativity.

1. I have replaced "thinking out of the box" with *Flick the Switch*. What word or phrase are you going to use?
2. In your own words, what is the difference between Creativity and Innovation? Think of three examples.
3. Sylvan Goldman invented the supermarket shopping trolley. Which two "Light Bulbs" (ideas) did he bring together to get his new idea?
4. List the areas of your job that require Creative Thinking and the areas that do not. Now do the same for your boss's job and your subordinate's job. What do you notice?
5. Now for a brain-teaser. If you have mastered the 9-dots game, try the 12-dot game. Connect these dots with only 5 straight lines without taking your pen off the paper.

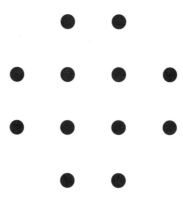

6. Too easy? Then try this with 6 straight lines. Keep that pen on the paper.

2
Why all the Fuss?

Q: How many board meetings does it take to get a light bulb changed?

A: This topic was resumed from last week's discussion, but is incomplete pending resolution of some action items. It will be continued next week. Meanwhile...

OK, so we've defined Creativity and Innovation. We understand the Light Bulbs. But why is there so much emphasis on Creativity these days? Wasn't there always a need to be creative?

Maybe the answer lies in the progress of human society. During various stages of man's development he has been encouraged or discouraged from being creative, depending on the circumstances surrounding him.

Let's go Back in Time

Primitive man had no choice but to be creative. To outwit an enemy. To catch an animal for lunch or to avoid being its lunch. To build a shelter from the weather. To make a stone tool.

As man progressed his creativity continued as he experimented with crops, domesticated animals and built civilizations on the banks of the great rivers like the Nile, Tigris and Euphrates.

But during the Middle Ages people were actively discouraged from original thought and progress slowed. A woman with a different way of thinking or doing things was called a witch and punished accordingly. A person who questioned the church's teachings was punished as a heretic. Not exactly an incentive for original thought.

Everything changed with the Industrial Revolution. The creative minds of the day invented new and better ways to produce things. But with the progress of mass production came low-level, repetitive factory jobs. The order of the industrial age became, *"Don't think – just do"*.

Perhaps those that left industrial Europe to make a fresh start in the new world kick-started a new wave of creativity. They had to be creative to overcome the problems they encountered as they went about their new life in a new place.

And the last century or so? A mix of unparalleled progress, mass education, rules and regulations, repetitive jobs, incredible life-saving inventions, exceeded only by life-taking ones. And the average man and woman? Now beginning to realise the necessity for more creative thinking.

The Competition is Hot

Competition is everywhere and hotter than ever. Students from very young ages compete for the highest marks and position in the class. As they get older, they compete for limited places in the best secondary schools, universities and business schools. Sometimes the competition they face to get in is tougher than the course itself.

You might be competing in the workplace for that next promotion, the next job offer, or a place on a committee. As Mark Bryan says, business *"...will increasingly reward those people who are able to be creative."*

Indeed, creative thinking might be the only legal and moral way for you to get ahead of the pack.

And no wonder employers are looking for more creative people. According to Dilip Mukerjea, creative people are more productive, profitable, effective, efficient and agile.

Speaking of business, in this fast-paced and fast-shrinking world, products are being copied by others across the globe in shorter and shorter times. Leaps in technology by one business are being copied by another or leapt right over. So businesses need to be constantly creative to remain competitive. They can't rest on their laurels.

And it doesn't stop there. Countries compete with each other in a huge global marketplace. These days a country's success may depend more and more on its ability to educate and equip a creative workforce than on its labour abundance or natural resources.

Take Singapore for example. No natural resources and an increasingly expensive labour force limit Singapore's ability to compete. Continued success can only come from more creative approaches to business and government. The Singapore government knows this and is doing all it can to build a creative and innovative society.

So we now live in a time when the real difference between people, businesses and countries lies in our ideas. All of us are being challenged to look for new and better ways of doing things. That requires Creative Thinking.

The ROIs of Creativity

Thinking Creatively requires extra effort, but there is a Return On the Investment. The ROI of creativity for individuals includes getting noticed, greater satisfaction, job promotion and higher income. For businesses it includes better procedures and policies, superior customer service, greater employee satisfaction and loyalty, improved products, bigger market share and higher profitability. For countries it includes better trade results, more economic activity and higher standards of living.

Creative Thinking enables individuals, businesses and countries to determine what they want to be and to create their own future rather than just having their future dictated to them by outside forces.

But there's a second ROI to creativity that is worth discussing. I am going to borrow that ROI from the advertising agency DDB Worldwide. They say that advertising needs to have Relevance, Originality and Impact. And I believe the same is true for Creativity in general.

Here are a few quotes from Bill Bernbach (the B in DDB) on DDB's ROI.

On Relevance: *"You are not right if in your ad you stand a man on his head just to get attention. You are right if you have him on his head to show how your product keeps things from falling out of his pockets."*

Similarly, for your creative idea to be valuable to your business, it must be relevant to the problem you are trying to solve. That is to say, your creative idea must also be strategically sound. Creativity for creativity's sake has little value except in the world of fine art. There will be lots of wonderful ideas that won't move you closer to achieving your objectives. Don't waste time on them.

On Originality: *"If your advertising goes unnoticed, everything else is academic."* and *"In communications, familiarity breeds apathy."*

How many times have you seen ads that look like other ads? Ads for banks that could be for *any* bank. Ads for computers that could be for *any* computer. Ads for retailers that could be for *any* store. These unoriginal ideas have a hard time getting noticed and an even harder time of being successful.

The same is true for your creative idea, whether it is for a new procedure at work or a way to ask your boss for a pay rise. If your idea isn't original it may not get the attention of the very people it is meant for.

But how original is original? Your idea doesn't have to be *totally* original. It might be an adaptation of someone else's idea.

But for it to be successful, you need to 'package it' so that people can see how you've made the idea work for your particular situation. You need to show them how the adaptation makes it original in your circumstances.

Is J.K. Rowling's *Harry Potter and the Sorcerer's Stone* – or any book for that matter – a totally original work? It can't be. There are plenty of books about boys. Books about wizards. Books about boarding school. Books about magic. And books about imaginary worlds. But J.K Rowling has woven all those themes together in a delightful way that makes her book original, yet not *totally* so.

If you strive for total originality, good luck. Because, as the saying goes – there is nothing new under the sun. There's only the merger of things that already exist.

But keep in mind that you'll have to sell your idea to someone. Perhaps you will have to sell it up the line, or to your staff, or a client or perhaps to the shareholders. In any case, if the idea seems too familiar, it might not get the attention of those you're hoping will buy it. They will have heard it all before and reject it.

I fell victim to this problem myself some years ago. I was working in an advertising agency in Australia. One of our clients only ever advertised in print, even though television advertising would have been far more effective. I remember trying to convince the client time and time again to switch to TV, but getting nowhere. Then, one day out of the blue, another agency met with our client and convinced them to advertise on TV. Instead of using the rational argument I had been preaching, they simply developed a

TV idea and showed it to the client. My opponents knew the value of presenting their idea in an attention-getting way and they got the result I failed to get.

So whatever your idea, package it in an original way to get the attention of your audience.

Now back to Bill…

On Impact Bill Bernbach said: *"Properly practiced creativity must result in greater sales more economically achieved."*

Bernbach was in the advertising business so he looked at creativity as the means to sell his clients' products. Whether you are trying to sell a product or not, the creative idea you generate must have the desired impact on the issue it is addressing. It has to get the result you were looking for in the first place.

It doesn't matter how creative your idea is, how relevant it is to your strategy and how original it is if it doesn't get the result it was designed to get.

Let's say, for example, you wanted to convince your client at the poultry farm that you are very creative. So you decide to wear a chicken on your head. It might be Relevant (they're in the poultry business). It might be Original (they haven't seen that before). But if it results in them thinking you are stupid instead of creative, it is the wrong thing to do. It has the wrong kind of Impact.

Effective creativity will give you a return on your intellectual investment. To be sure it is effective, check it against DDB's guidelines – Relevance, Originality and Impact. But remember that two out of three isn't good enough. You need all three.

Don't Go Overboard

Not everyone needs to be creative in their job all
the time. There comes a time when we know
what to do and we should just do it. Imagine
if the young man cooking a Big Mac at
McDonald's decided to be creative with it. He
might try to cook it for longer; squash it flatter;
add some celery and beetroot; forget the cheese. We
as customers would never be sure of what we were
going to get. And McDonald's wouldn't have the consistency that
built its brand.

Some jobs require us to do the same thing in exactly the same
way and to the exact same standards every time. Any job in mass
production is like that.

But behind all those jobs was the Creative stage when the idea
first emerged and the Innovation was put into practice. Like the
time when the Big Mac was introduced by Jim Delligatti. He and
his team decided everything about it from the ingredients to the
cooking time to the name.

However, even if we have a successful formula like the Big
Mac, we can't stand back and let the ways of the past continue
forever. The world moves and we need to move with it. And that
is precisely why McDonald's is now introducing several new items
to its menu.

If we keep doing things the same way we will soon be overrun by
competitors who have better ideas. So continually review your habits,
products and procedures and only keep them if they are better than the
best alternative that you can create.

Everyday Creativity

Other jobs require us to be Creative for much of the time. Like when we're dealing with people. Or selling. When we're building a brand. Writing ads. Outsmarting a competitor. Making a presentation. Refining a business model. Developing a business strategy. Formulating a policy. Determining a pricing strategy. Selecting a new employee. Negotiating with a customer or with a staff member.

And we can all exercise Creativity in our personal lives. Writing an email. Dealing with our children. Planning our financial future. Enjoying our spare time. Organising a holiday. Surprising a loved-one. Re-arranging the furniture. Decorating a Christmas tree. Cooking a meal. Buying an outfit. Tending a garden. Choosing a radio station. The list is endless.

One More Reason for Creativity

And if all that isn't good reason enough to be more Creative, consider this one: *it's simply more fun.* You can choose to live a boring, repetitive life. Or you can choose to stretch your mind and find new ways to do things. Try new activities. Tackle problems in different ways. No-one else can *flick your creative switch.*

It's up to you.

Lighten Up

Try these few exercises to lighten up your life.

1. Write down the advantages to you of being more creative in your work and in your personal life. Find at least seven advantages for each.

2. Write down five jobs where creativity is potentially harmful. Why?

3. On a scale of one to 10, where one is Homer Simpson and ten is Marilyn vos Savant, how intelligent are you? (Marilyn vos Savant has the highest ever recorded IQ.)

4. Now on a scale of one to 10, where one is a bicycle and 10 is a Ferrari, how creative are you?

5. What do you think questions three and four are trying to tell you? Make at least three observations.

6. Take a look at your current CV. Does your creative ability show through in the way it is written or in the achievements you have listed? If not, fix it.

3
Everyone's Creative…
Or at least it can be

Q: How many visitors to an art gallery does it take to screw in a light bulb?

A: Two. One to do it and one to say "Huh ! My four-year old could've done that!"

At the end of the last chapter I suggested you rate yourself on how creative you are. We do the same thing in our workshops. We've heard the full range of scores and we've also had answers like Skateboard and Gogomobile. (Maybe they're trying to think out of the Boxster.) Interestingly we find that many people rate their creative abilities quite low.

I Can't Draw

When we ask them to explain their reasoning we hear answers like these:

> *I can't draw; I can't sing; I can't write; I can't paint;*
> *I can't play an instrument; I can't act; Can't this and*
> *can't that!*

What about all the things they can do? We'll come back to this.

When we work with people in creative industries, like advertising, we get different answers. People rate themselves much higher on creativity. Not surprisingly, you might say.

But let's get behind this. I don't think the advertising people are saying they are creative because they can sing, paint, play an instrument or act. Sure some of them are good at art and writing, but those in the Account Management department don't usually do these things. So what's happening? Are all the creative people drawn to the creative industries? Do the creative industries bring out the creativity in people? Do the people in creative industries have a different view of creativity? Maybe all three.

Roger von Oech, in his book "A Whack on the Side of the Head" tells of a study by a major oil company to find what differentiated creative people from the less creative ones. The study found that the creative people thought they were creative, and the less creative people thought they weren't. So those who thought they weren't creative never tried to use their creativity. The self-fulfilling prophesy in action.

Overhaul Your Definition

So it would seem, your ability to be creative is largely in your mind – which makes sense, seeing that's where Creativity starts anyway. A good way to empower your creative-self is to overhaul your definition of what is creative.

It's a given that drawing, painting, writing, dancing, movies, theatre and music are creative. But let's go further.

We already said that Creativity is "the merging of ideas which have not been merged before". So you are being creative when you:

- Have any original idea
- Use an old idea in a new way
- Express yourself to help someone understand something
- Use your imagination to visualize the future
- Anticipate someone's objections to your sales pitch
- Use an analogy or metaphor
- Make a pun
- Extend or expand on another person's idea
- Improvise when you don't have the right tools or materials
- Change a recipe to suit your sense of taste
- Make up a story to tell your children
- Imagine a picture in a cloud

- Organise a filing system
- Rearrange the furniture
- Dance, however badly
- Try a different route to avoid a traffic jam

Of course there are thousands of creative acts and you do many of them every day.

Having a broader definition of Creativity might give us greater belief in our creative abilities. But there are still things that stop us from reaching our creative potential.

What Stops Us?

We are the result of everything that ever happened to us in our lives. Everything we ever experienced. Let's just look at some of the things we've been told and how they may have stifled our Creativity.

We have heard, *don't be foolish, grow up, work before play, do as you're told, don't ask questions, obey the rules, be practical,* and many other limiting phrases. The truth is that these all get in the way of creative thinking.

Don't be foolish

"Don't be foolish," "grow up" and "work before play" tell us that we should be serious. Yet we know that the mind is most creative when it's at play. If we try to be creative but don't allow our mind into its fertile playground we prevent ourselves from seeing anything but grown-up solutions. We look for logic and we self-censor. But by playing the fool we may discover new ways of seeing things that might help us develop new ideas. So be foolish. Play. Be a child. It will help you think more creatively.

Do as you're told

"Do as you're told" and "obey the rules" prevent us from thinking about things for ourselves. We see it in adults who blindly follow rules without even knowing why the rules exist. Then once a situation arises that doesn't quite fit the rules, they don't know what to do. And customers are told things like: "It's our policy", "We always do it like that", "Everyone does it that way". It shows a complete lack of understanding and original thought and it is frustrating for customers to be told such things.

When someone tells me their company's policy and it doesn't suit my needs, I tell them I have a policy too. My policy is not to accept anyone else's policy unless it has a valid reason that applies to my particular situation. I usually get referred to a supervisor who is allowed to think.

Rather than blindly follow the rules, figure out why they are there in the first place. Then you will be able to determine whether they are valid when different circumstances arise. And if not, you will be able to bend the rules to something more appropriate.

Don't ask questions

Sometimes in our workshops we set assignments and give people a time limit like 8 minutes and 12 seconds. We are amazed that most people aren't even curious about such a time limit. At some point in their lives their curiosity was killed. When we lose our curiosity or become afraid to ask questions, we stop ourselves from expanding our mind and, as we will see later, that prevents us from finding connections that bring about new ideas.

Life will hit you with plenty of problems and opportunities (Light Bulb #1s) to deal with. And the more information (Light Bulb #2s) you have in your head, the more potential connections you'll be able to make to address those issues creatively. So be curious, read widely, look, listen and build your knowledge. Ask questions.

Be practical

"Be practical" is yet another way of conditioning us to limit our imagination and ability to explore unusual possibilities. When looking for creative solutions we need to put aside all thoughts of being practical. Explore the impractical and even the impossible because they may lead you to a new area of thought.

Don't be foolish, grow up, work before play, do as you're told, don't ask questions, obey the rules, be practical, are just some of the negative things we've been told. Although they may have been said to us with the best of intentions, they limit our creative abilities.

So here are two things for you to do. First, delete those phrases from your mind… don't let them limit you any longer. And second, stop perpetuating the problem. Bite your tongue when you are tempted to say them to other people.

Blame your school?

While at school we soon learned that the way to get the teacher's approval was to guess what was in his or her mind. By answering questions the way the teacher wanted, we were rewarded with high marks, smiles and a good report. Unfortunately that taught us two very bad, uncreative habits.

First, it taught us to second-guess our superiors instead of figuring things out for ourselves. We soon found that the best answer in school was the one the teacher wanted. At work, there's a tendency to come up with the answer we think the boss wants to hear. This behaviour just creates yes-men and yes-women. It doesn't take thinking anywhere new. It perpetuates the status quo.

Second, school taught us to look only as far as one right answer. We stopped searching once we found that one right answer instead of looking for the second right answer or third right answer. Unlike mathematics, there are multiple right answers for every business situation. Look beyond the first right answer to the less obvious and more creative answers.

To *flick the creative switch* we need to rid ourselves of the preconditioning that stifles free thinking and find the things that stimulate us to think more creatively. But don't just blame your school. You're an adult now. You can think and behave the way you choose.

So What Starts Us?

Now it's time to get positive and think of all the things that help us with Creative Thinking.

Not too many of us get up in the morning and say to ourselves, "I think I'll be creative today". Instead, we go to work and face situations that require solutions. But we *can* make a choice on how creatively we approach those problems. And some things, more than others, prompt us towards more creative solutions.

You Are What You EAT

You've heard the phrase before. It is not totally original, but I will *flick my switch* and use it an an original way. I believe that our creativity depends on three things:

the Environment, our Attitude and the creative thinking Tools we use. Let's start with Environment.

Environment

First, the <u>external environment</u>.

It is said that necessity is the mother of invention, and I guess that makes sense. (Would we have invented umbrellas if it never rained?) Necessity was certainly the driver for the inventions of the pioneers who faced life-threatening hardships and had to find ways to survive. Although we don't find the same hardships these days, there are modern day business equivalents.

Consider the automobile industry and the development of safer cars. Would the manufacturers have poured countless millions of dollars into safer car designs if it were not for safety legislation? Probably not. And now the emphasis is on fossil-free fuels and it is redirecting creative efforts in the same industry. When governments or other regulating bodies place pressures on us they are acting as the mothers of invention.

And for you? When your shareholders demand higher returns, when your customers demand better service, when the unions demand better working conditions, when your competitors begin to poach your best people, when your rivals leapfrog your product... these are your mothers of invention.

These influences on your creativity are environmental, but external to you. The internal environment also has a significant influence on your creativity.

So let's turn our attention to your internal environment.

Imagine trying NOT to be creative if you worked for MTV, Saatchi & Saatchi, Pixar, Disney, Virgin or Apple. How successful could you be? How comfortable would you feel? How long would you last?

When you work for a creative organisation, the environment itself is creative and creativity breeds more creativity. Of course the opposite is true too. It's extremely difficult to be the only one trying to do creative things in an organisation that doesn't appreciate or understand creativity. If you want to improve your creativity, find creative people within your business and mix with them. You can encourage each other.

Even the physical environment can influence your creativity. Visual and aural stimuli, the level of physical comfort, degree of stress, and laughter are known to have an influence on our creativity. But the influence can vary from person to person.

To improve your creativity you need to figure out what environmental factors help you and then put them in place. For example, some people can't concentrate if there's background music. Others might be at their most creative when Ozzy Osbourne is pounding out on the stereo. Do what works for you. Just be aware that what you do may impact on others. If their needs differ from yours, work with them to come up with a creative solution.

Attitude

You can't do something you don't want to do, don't believe in or don't believe you can. On the other hand, as Paul Meyer, founder of Success Motivation Institute said, *"Whatever you vividly imagine, ardently desire, sincerely believe, and enthusiastically act upon... must inevitably come to pass!"*

Kind of says it all, doesn't it?

Tools

So you've got the right attitude – you're all fired up. The internal environment is conducive to creativity – you've painted the walls yellow, pictures of Einstein and Nicole Kidman are all over the office and the stereo's playing the Pink Floyd classic 'Dark Side of the Moon'. The external environment is demanding creative solutions. In fact, your brand's survival depends on it. There's just one thing missing:

You don't know how to be creative.

For some people creativity comes naturally. They never seem to struggle with it. Often they don't even know where their ideas come from. They just seem to happen.

If you're not one of them, don't worry. There are tools you can use that will allow you to employ the same thought processes that creative people use naturally. In other words, you can learn tools that will force you towards creative solutions. Because the important thing to know is HOW to think rather than WHAT to think.

Part Two of this book will introduce you to a number of tools and show you how to use them for everyday business situations. When you've mastered them, you will begin to use them naturally, without even going through the processes.

So you see, everyone is creative, or at least can be. *Flick your creative switch* by overhauling your definition of what is Creative. Delete all those self-limiting phrases from your memory and replace them with the right attitude. Work out your environmental stimuli, learn and practice the creative tools and you can become a truly creative thinker.

Try These

Get comfortable (if that helps), tell yourself you can do these, and give it a try.

1. List all the things you have been told that have stifled your creative abilities. Now think of anything else that may have interfered with your creative confidence. What can you do to stop them limiting you in the future?

2. Think about when you are most creative. Can you identify the stimuli that help you? How can you replicate or increase those stimuli?

3. Make a list of at least 20 creative things you have done in the last three months, however small. Use the list on pages 31 and 32 to help you.

4. What is the one most successful creative thing you have done in your life? Recall how you felt when you did it.

5. Consider your place of work. What external and internal factors are forcing your company to re-examine its products, services or procedures?

6. Now for something completely different: Why are manhole covers round? Find at least three good reasons.

4

Inside Your Head

Q: How many psychiatrists does it take to change a light bulb?

A: Only one, but the light bulb must want to change.

This is going to be a very unscientific chapter. I am not a scientist, neurologist or biologist. And in any case, while the brain is the most studied part of our bodies it is the least understood. Anything scientific we print here is likely to be outdated while you're still reading it. So let's take a lay-view.

Left Versus Right

You have probably read that the brain is divided into two hemispheres. They are actually two different brains joined by the Corpus Callosum. It's via this Corpus Callosum that the two halves 'talk' to each other.

The Left and Right sides have different functions. Studies measuring brain waves while people think about different things indicate that each side of the brain handles the following mental activities:

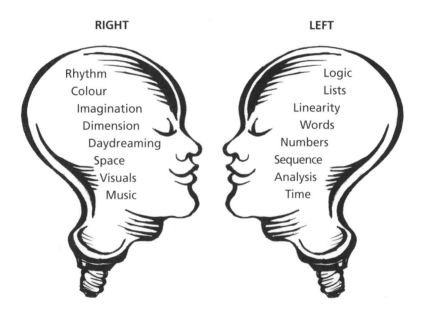

RIGHT

Rhythm
Colour
Imagination
Dimension
Daydreaming
Space
Visuals
Music

LEFT

Logic
Lists
Linearity
Words
Numbers
Sequence
Analysis
Time

Interestingly the left side lists the sorts of things we normally associate with "brainy" people. The right side list contains the things we traditionally think of as creative. The truth is, both sides of the brain are creative. Remember that we overhauled our definition of Creativity? Language is creative, science is creative, writing is creative... just as art is creative.

Take a Closer Look

The brain is not just two lumps of gray matter sitting neatly inside your head. In fact, it isn't even gray. Unless you're dead, it's pink. So now you can replace that phrase, "Use your gray matter" with *"Use your pink matter"*.

Your brain is incredibly complicated, being composed of millions of tiny cells called neurons. We have about 10 billion neurons and each is kind of like a tiny octopus with lots of little tentacles. According to Tony Buzan each of these tentacles has *"thousands of tiny protuberances, much like the suction pads on the tentacles of the octopus, but protruding from all sides of the tentacle."*

The tentacles are connected to other tentacles through electrochemical impulses and it's these connections or pathways that allow us to think creatively when we link one thing to another. The more unusual the link, the more creative we consider the thought.

World's Biggest Filing Cabinet

Think of your brain as a huge filing cabinet where you store information. As you see, hear or use any of your senses, your mind neatly puts the information in the filing cabinet in its proper drawer. Sometimes this filing takes place in our sleep. While our conscious mind is resting, our subconscious mind gets busy making sense out of the day's activities and tidies everything away. That's why a complex issue always seems clearer in the morning. That's why we say, "Let me sleep on it".

So the link between the filing cabinet and the tentacles? Those little tentacles are the drawers in the world's biggest filing cabinet – your brain.

Everything's Connected

Take a look around you. Everything you see is connected to everything else, even if it's just that you can see them. But look more closely and you'll find that whatever two things you compare, there are other deeper or less obvious connections.

Let's try connecting these two things: pizzas and personal relationships. Start by examining the one most easily understood and finding similarities or new thoughts for the second. Most people (especially men) would understand pizzas better than relationships, so let's start there.

1. Pizzas are round. So are healthy personal relationships. Are your relationships round? How can you make your relationships rounder?
2. Pizzas have a base. So must personal relationships. What is the basis of your relationship with the person who is closest to you?

3. Pizzas have toppings to add flavour. These are like the many aspects or dimensions of a relationship. Is yours a bland relationship or one with many toppings?
4. Pizzas need heat. Relationships need heat too. How can you heat-up your relationships?
5. Pizzas come in many types: Hawaiian, Quattro Fromaggi, Napolitana, The Works, etc. There are many types of personal relationships. Family, friends, lovers, neighbours and business, for example.
6. Pizzas are for sharing. Relationships are about sharing. Do you have a sharing relationship?
7. Pizzas take some work, but are essentially easy. Your relationships take work, but they should not be too hard to maintain. If they're difficult, something's wrong.
8. Pizzas are satisfying. Worthwhile relationships are satisfying too.

These are all fairly straight forward. Here are three more aspects of pizzas that you might be able to connect with personal relationships.

- Pizzas can be sliced
- Pizzas are quick
- Pizzas come in doughy crust and crispy crust.

We could go on and draw more parallels but I'm getting hungry, so let's stop talking about food and try a different example.

Let's connect a compact disk and a business card. This time we'll go one step further and see if we can generate some new ideas from the connection.

First, both are sitting on my desk. But both also have the following in common:

-   They belong to me
-   They are both rectangular
-   They are colourful
-   They contain writing
-   They feature the name of their 'sponsor'
-   They reflect the personality of the owner
-   They have been carefully designed
-   They can be thrown
-   And so on.

Looking for connections goes further than spotting what things have in common. It also includes their differences. Consider the CD and the business card. The CD case:

-   Is fragile
-   Can be opened
-   Is bigger than the business card
-   Contains a booklet about the singer and the songs
-   Has a picture of the artist, etc.

The CD itself:

-   Is round
-   Needs a CD player to work
-   Is shiny
-   Contains songs
-   Has a hole in the middle

Meanwhile the business card:

-   Is flatter and lighter than the CD
-   Is more easily stored

- Can be folded
- Shows your personal contact details
- Can be reproduced cheaply enough to give away.

If we use our knowledge of the similarities and differences we can challenge what a business card or a CD and its case <u>could</u> be like. For example: Could we... put your picture or some other picture on your business card? Make it out of plastic? Have it fold open? Make it round like the CD? Put a hole in the middle? Make it a mini CD? Make it talk or sing? Link it to your website? Make it a booklet about you and your company?

Could the CD case be more flexible? Shatterproof? Flatter? One piece instead of two?

Could the CD be 'disposable'? Smaller? More durable so that the case isn't needed? Linked to the singer's website? Linked to an online music store?

You can see where this is heading. We can use all of these ideas to get even more ideas.

In later chapters we'll look at how to connect things that are seemingly unconnected. For now, all you have to do is believe that everything is connected to everything else and that, given enough brain power, you can make the connection and get new ideas.

Using the Light Bulbs

The Light Bulbs we introduced earlier are your visual cues to how to think more creatively. Each Light Bulb represents a different area of your brain, where you hold information relating to a particular topic.

Let Light Bulb #1 always represent the issue you are facing. So it will contain the facts and feelings about the topic under review, including your desire to change something. It might all be neatly tucked away in one little filing drawer or you may have to open a few filing drawers to get all the facts and feelings together. In any case, Light Bulb #1 represents the status quo. We might also call it 'the brief'.

If you focus your attention solely on Light Bulb #1 you will have difficulty coming up with creative solutions. Your brain will try its best to remain in the same filing cabinet drawer and the solutions you come up with will be logical and predictable. A bit like thinking inside the box.

To *flick your creative switch* we need Light Bulb #2. It's our creative stimulus. But where is it?

It's in a different section of the world's biggest filing cabinet. We find a new filing cabinet drawer far removed from the first one – completely unrelated. We open the drawer and take out Light Bulb #2. It will be the stimulus to help us think differently. Then all you need do is force the connection between the two Light Bulbs and find creative ways to approach your issue, just as we forced ourselves to connect pizzas and personal relationships.

You see, whether we seem better with our left or our right brain, we can still be creative. To be more creative, we just have to find ways to connect things in our minds that are not usually connected, whether both are on the left, both are on the right or one is on each side of our brain. Then we force ourselves to find the similarities or differences that enable us to expand our ideas.

Of course, if we fill our heads with more information and experiences and if we learn to think better with both sides of our brain, there will be even more opportunities for those creative connections.

Exponential Creative Potential

Remember the Creativity formula $C = (ME)^\infty$ we discussed in Chapter 1? We said that C = Creativity; M = mass of data, information, knowledge and wisdom acquired over your lifetime; and E = the sum of Experiences and the Enlightenment gained thereby, that serve to Energise your life.

Let's put it to the test. Follow me with this calculation of creative potential....

If you only have two things in your brain, you can only make one connection. If you add one new experience (or new fact), you have three possible connections. Adding a fourth experience takes the potential connection count to six. Five experiences...10 connections. Now look what happens as we add more and more experiences and/or knowledge:

Experiences/Knowledge	Potential Connections
10	45
50	1,225
100	4,950
1,000	499,500
10,000	49,995,000
100,000	4,999,950,000
1,000,000	499,999,500,000
10,000,000	49,999,995,000,000

You can see the exponential growth in potential connections when we add new information and new experiences. Obviously, the more you read, see, do, taste, feel, smell and hear, the more creative you can become. It grows exponentially towards infinity.

That's why your creative potential can increase with age. Age itself doesn't stop creativity as many people think. It's attitude that prevents many older people from living up to their creative potential. (Or it might be Alzheimer's. I forget which.)

So fill the world's biggest filing cabinet inside your head, *flick your creative switch* and force those creative connections.

Connect These

1. Look at the list of Left and Right brain activities on page 42 and of the 16 listed there, choose the six you are best at. What do you notice about your style of thinking? Left, Right or rather Balanced?

2. Consider whether the most creative people are Left brained, Right brained or Balance brained. Why do you think that?

3. What does a ladder have in common with a strategic plan? Find at least five things.

4. How can you take what you know about flowers and apply it to improving team work in your office?

5. What do water and calculators have in common? Find at least three things.

6. Pick up a common everyday paperclip. Force your mind out of its 'paperclip/stationery' filing cabinet drawer and find 20 other uses for a paperclip.

7. Connect your understanding of Creativity with your sense of smell. What does Creativity smell like? Why do you think that?

5
Pathways of Habit

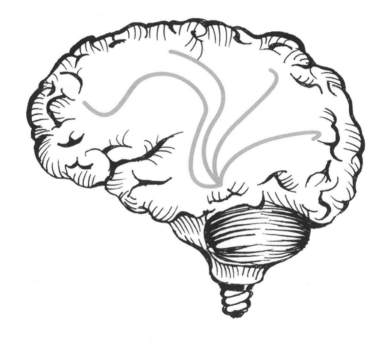

Q: How many bureaucrats does it take to screw in a light bulb?

A: Two. One to assure everyone that everything possible is being done while the other screws the bulb into the water faucet.

"Who am I? I am your constant companion.
I am your greatest helper or heaviest burden.
I will push you onwards or drag you down to failure.
I am completely at your command.

"Half the things you do you might just as well turn
over to me and I will do them quickly and correctly.
I am easily managed, you must merely be firm with me.

"Show me exactly how you want something done and
after a few lessons I will do it automatically.
I am the servant of all great men and women and,
alas, of all failures as well.

"Those who are great, I have made great. Those who
are failures, I have made failures.
I am not a machine, though I work with the precision
of a machine, plus the intelligence of a person.

"You may run me for profit or run me for ruin, it
makes no difference to me. Take me, train me, be firm
with me, and I will place the world at your feet.

Be easy with me and I will destroy you.

"Who am I? I am Habit." - Gary Kroehnert

In the last chapter we talked about connecting things in our minds. The connections form 'pathways' and those pathways, when used often, are easily navigated. The things we tend to do frequently, become habits. And as you can see from the above, a habit is a two-edged sword.

Let's think some more about habits by looking at what others have said about them:

"A habit is the intersection of knowledge, skill and desire."
– Stephen Covey.

"We are what we repeatedly do. Excellence, then, is not an act, but a habit."
– Aristotle.

"People do not really decide their future... they decide their habits – then their habits decide their future."
– Unknown.

The Duke of Wellington, in response to the question of whether habit is second nature, replied *"Second nature? It's ten times nature!"*

It's quite clear that habits play an enormous role in our lives. If we are to understand the Creative Habit, then we must first understand habits, where they come from and the pathways they form in our minds.

99% Or More

Habits are acquired. We're not born with them. Every experience contributes to our habit formation. From the moment we are born we have been making and breaking habits and forming new ones. By the time we reach adulthood most of our life's habits are well entrenched.

Perhaps the man who had the most to say about habits was the psychologist and philosopher William James (1842-1910). One particularly sobering thing James said was *"Ninety-nine hundredths or, possibly nine hundred and ninety-nine thousandths of our activity is purely automatic and habitual, from our rising in the morning to our lying down at night."*

We all know how powerful habits can be. I particularly like this story of David Hilbert, the German mathematician, also famous for his absent-mindedness…

During a party at Hilbert's house, his wife noticed that he had neglected to put on a clean shirt. She sent him upstairs to change. When, after 10 minutes he hadn't returned she went to check what had happened. She found him asleep in bed. Evidently, habit had taken control. He had taken off his coat, then his tie, then his shirt. So naturally, he went to bed.

Now that may not have happened to us, but habits are an important part of our very existence. Imagine if we woke every morning and had to re-learn how to get out of bed, where the bathroom is, how to button our clothes or how to make breakfast. Imagine shaving "for the first time" every time. We'd never leave home. By giving over much of our lives to habits, we are free to explore other more important things.

Done Often, Done Easily

When we try to do something for the first time it might be difficult, but if we persevere we get better at it. We say that practice makes perfect because we know that things done often are done more and more easily. The more often we do something the more worn the pathway in our mind becomes. Then after a while our mind goes down that newly formed pathway of habit without thinking about it. The new thing becomes automatic. Like driving a car.

When you first commence learning to drive, it all seems impossible. There's so much to remember, so much to watch out for. But once you master it, you drive without giving a second's thought to gear changes, turn signals, the rear view mirror and all those other things that frightened you on that first day you sat behind the wheel. All those actions become habits as the pathways become well defined.

So all this sounds like habits are good.

But I can hear you thinking, *what about bad habits?* We all have them. Whether it is over-eating, over-drinking, smoking, worrying excessively, spending too much money, thinking the worst about people, watching too much TV, doubting our abilities or maybe trying to please others. These are things we call bad habits and they're the sort of things that new year's resolutions are designed to counter.

Bad habits are the well worn pathways of the *ineffective* things we do. Those behaviours may once have given us satisfaction. After a time they no longer serve their original purpose yet we keep doing them. As children we put off doing our homework until, at the last minute, Mummy helped us. We subconsciously learnt that if we put off doing difficult things, someone would come to our rescue. This is one of the ways the procrastination habit is born. So habits are good *and* bad.

When we're under stress we revert to our basic habits, even if rationally we know them to be ineffective. Our habits bring comfort because it's far easier to do something in a way we have before than to force ourselves to try something new. We often stay with our habits because we fear that an untried way of doing things will fail. Or because our experience with the alternative is worse than with the habit. We say, "better the devil you know".

We need to be certain that when we approach any problem or situation, we don't automatically follow the same habitual path, because in the wrong hands (or more accurately, the wrong brain) our habits can lead us to unsatisfactory conclusions. They can stop us looking for the second, third and fourth right answer. They can lead to results that are unimaginative, boring, expected, unoriginal and safe. The very opposites to Creative.

Holding on to Habits

Often our habits don't lead us to the results we want, yet we hold on to them. Are we expecting some sort of miracle that the same old actions will somehow produce better results? This, I am told, is the definition of insanity.

There's a saying that goes, "If you do things the way you've always done them, you'll get the same results you've always got". It sounds reasonable, but it assumes everything else has remained constant. The world is changing rapidly and the habits we developed in the past are less and less likely to be appropriate today or in the future. Try replacing that saying with this one:

If you do things the way you've always done them you'll get WORSE RESULTS THAN YOU EVER GOT!

We all have to find better ways of doing things and old thoughts, like "if it ain't broke, don't fix it" and "leave well enough alone" are stopping us from moving forward.

Certainly we need some habits to help us live without the stress of re-learning every moment of our lives, but are we also holding on to some ineffective old habits? Or to habits that, although effective, are less effective than some new behaviours might be?

Breaking Old Habits

Stephen Covey talks about the gravity of habits. He says that habits have a pull on us, much like gravity's pull. He says that breaking deeply imbedded habits requires more than just willpower. It actually requires tremendous effort. But we can all do it.

Covey says that change is a painful process that *"has to be motivated by a higher purpose, by the willingness to subordinate what you think you want now for what you want later"*.

Some theories of habits state that a habit can't be broken unless it is replaced with another. We can't go back through our lives and replace the experiences that caused our negative habits. But we can displace those experiences with new experiences and attitudes. Remember, we are what we EAT. Attitude is up to us. If we tell ourselves positive things repeatedly we can displace old attitudes and the old negative habits associated with them.

The Creative Habit

Now here's a conundrum about habits. If doing things by habit means doing things the same way every time, and being creative is doing things differently every time, is it possible or useful to make Creative Thinking a habit? I believe the answer to both is *yes*.

First, it is possible to make Creative Thinking a habit. Creative Thinking is behaviour so, like other behaviours, it can be learned, practiced and mastered, done often and done easily.

Second, the big advantage is that Creative Thinking doesn't lead to the same results every time. It leads to *Creative results*. It gets you into the habit of finding creative solutions to problems. That is because, as we said earlier, Creative Thinking is about HOW you think, not WHAT you think.

In *The Act of Creation*, Arthur Koestler sums it all up when he says, *"The greater mastery and ease we gain in the exercise of a skill, the more automized it will tend to become."* In other words, if you master the creative skills outlined in this book, the more automatic they will become. You will develop the Creative Habit.

All you have to do is believe in yourself, learn how to think creatively and do it at every opportunity. As William James said, *"We must make automatic and habitual, as early as possible, as many useful actions as we can."*

If you agree that Creative Thinking is useful, then why not make it a habit? And start now.

The Secret: The Stimulus

If you are like most people, when you have to address an issue, whether it be a problem or an opportunity, you do just that: you address *the issue*. You focus all your attention on the problem or on the opportunity.

When you do that you hinder creativity. Your mind searches for logical answers along its traditional pathways of habit. And you don't allow your subconscious mind to help you.

So the trick is NOT to focus on the situation, but instead to think about something else. Then you force yourself to find the link between that other thing and the situation you are addressing. It sounds like magic. And it is. That's what makes it creative.

Let's put it another way… if you come at an issue from a different starting point, you should get a different ending point. The different starting point is simply a stimulus. Remember the Light Bulbs? We're talking now about Light Bulb #2.

You'll recall that Light Bulb #1 is the current situation. Light Bulb #2, our stimulus, is another thing we know, but it is completely unrelated to the first thing. When we think creatively we can find the link between the two Light Bulbs and find creative answers. Those answers are Light Bulb #3.

Force Your New Pathways

When you do this, you are forcing a new pathway in your mind. If you continually challenge yourself to *flick your creative switch* you will get better and better at it. And you will form the Creative Habit. In Part II we'll see how to do it.

Examine Your Habits

Now it's time to take a look at your habits. Try these questions:

1. List down your five best habits. Can you think of when or why you adopted them? Who influenced you? What are the results of these habits? How satisfied are you with them?

2. Now do the same for your five worst habits.

3. Think about your workplace and identify the habits of your corporate culture. Which are good and which are bad? Which bad ones can you influence? How?

Now Stretch Your Brain

Like the muscles in your body, your mind needs exercise. Try this to tone up your most important muscle.

In this game you turn one word into another by changing one letter at each step. For example, I can turn DOG into CAT in three steps.

DOG
DOT
COT
CAT

Your exercise is to turn WORK into PLAY in the minimum number of steps. Good luck.

PART II

Kick-start Your Creative Habit

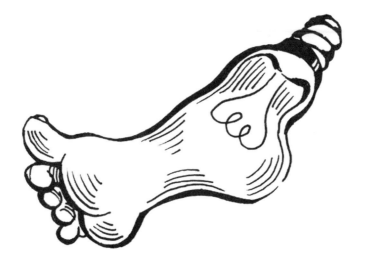

Q: How many art directors does it take to change a light bulb?

A: Does it have to be a light bulb?

In the remainder of this book I will introduce you to six tools that will help you *flick your creative switch*. The tools range from the simple to the complex, from ones you can use alone to ones that are best employed in teams.

Each tool is an example of Light Bulb #2 and, when applied to Light Bulb #1, should lead you or your team to creative solutions. They will give you a different starting point from which to tackle the issues you wish to address.

I will explain how each tool works, give you an example or two and then I will provide you with some questions or topics that might be dealt with using each particular tool.

There are just a couple of words of advice I'd like to offer you before you try the tools.

1. These tools might seem strange and you might be tempted to think they can't work. Try to stop yourself from thinking they are silly. Enjoy using them. And if you're really skeptical, just pretend they work and try them anyway.
2. Believe in yourself. You can find the connections that lead to original thought if you just apply yourself. Tell yourself positive things.
3. Persevere. If you don't get the results you're looking for at the first attempt, don't give up. Like all things, these tools require practice.
4. Write down every idea you get no matter how strange.
5. Suspend judgment. Instead of self-censoring, separate your creative thinking sessions from your evaluation sessions.
6. Don't expect that every idea is worth implementing. Idea generation is just the first step. Don't forget the Validation step before implementing any idea you come up with.

Now, let's *flick our switches*.

6
Random Word

Q: How many WWE wrestlers does it take
to change a light bulb?

A: Three. One to yank out the old bulb, throw it on the floor,
try to jump onto it from a great height, and act really surprised
when it rolls out of the way at the last minute. One to pretend
to twist the new one in round and round so far it almost breaks.
And some guy in a black and white stripy uniform whose
function is never made quite clear, to protest about something
or other, to the complete indifference of the bulb changers.

Random Word is a tool that is easily mastered and one that people usually enjoy using. Here's how it works.

We need a stimulus or Light Bulb #2. In this case it is a word prompt. We get the word randomly so that our biases or preconceived ideas will not influence our thought processes. Once we have the word, we then *flick our switch* by forcing ourselves to find the link between it and the issue we are facing.

The Best Random Words

The best words are nouns because they can be visualized. They have features and benefits that can be analysed. Abstract words and negative words are harder to deal with.

To understand what I am getting at, try visualizing 'conscience' or 'superfluous'. Contrast the difference between those abstract words and 'frying pan' or 'didgeridoo'.

So start by getting a tangible noun. Here's how you can do it.

Getting a Word

Notice that I have said "getting" a word and not "choosing" a word. We have to keep it random. Here are a few methods to get your word:

– Pick up a book or magazine and choose a page number. Then your word will be the first tangible noun on that page. Just be sure you choose a book or magazine that is not related to your topic. Try it now.
– Close your eyes and tell yourself the word will be the first red thing you see when you open your eyes. (It doesn't have to be red.)

– Choose a letter between A and E, and a number between one and 30. Then turn to the Random Words on page 73 to find your word. The first number is the column and the second number is the row. For example C12 is Flag.
– Visit www.creativeswitch.com and use the Random Word generator.
– Or make up some other method. Something that's fun.

Features and Benefits

Once you have your word, focus all your attention on it. Forget Light Bulb #1 for now. Interrogate your Random Word by listing down all the Features and all the Benefits of the word. Features are the physical attributes of the noun and benefits are what those features do for you. There's no need to try to match up particular benefits to particular features. Just let your mind go.

Give yourself a five minute time limit for this.

After you've listed all the features and benefits, you then start to force links between them and the issue you wish to address. Write down all the ideas that come to mind – no matter how silly – and, as always, separate idea generation from judgment.

Here's an example that came up in a workshop in Taiwan.

Random Example

The group was an advertising agency and their client was a brewery. Their challenge was to come up with new ideas to market BEER. The scope was as wide as they wanted to take it. All of the Marketing Ps were open to them: product, price, promotion and place. Plus positioning.

I gave them the Random Word "stereo". The Light Bulbs were these:

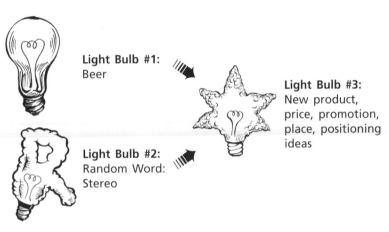

Light Bulb #1:
Beer

Light Bulb #2:
Random Word:
Stereo

Light Bulb #3:
New product,
price, promotion,
place, positioning
ideas

Here is a sample of what they came up with. Note that the features and benefits listed are not necessarily linked to each other.

Features	Benefits
Sound	Fun
CDs	Party
Tapes	Dating
Radio	Loud
Electric	Dancing
Volume control	Exercise with

Music	Stimulating
Tone	Clubs
Remote control	Sharing
Loud	Personal
Two channels	Relaxing
Black	Go anywhere
Portable	Attention getting

The list was longer, but you're getting the picture, right?

Then they tried to link these things to beer. Some of the links turned out to be difficult, but eventually they came to a wonderful idea. They would recommend a new beer targeted to younger adults, say 21 to 25 years of age. They'd let the older brands keep the older drinkers. They'd make this beer trendy and exclusive. Like this:

Positioning: For the younger, trendy, clubbing set, this is the beer that speaks, or rather *sings* your language. Reposition other beers as "Dad's beer".

Product: A bottled beer with a range of distinctive flavours like micro-brewery beers. A slightly lighter alcohol content because younger drinkers are less experienced with alcohol. Each of the six brews to represent six different types of music. Heavy Rock, Pop, Folk, Jazz, Rap and Hip Hop.

The bottle labels to reflect the music theme. Zany, colourful graphics like those used by MTV.

Price: Premium price in line with the image created.

Place: Only at pubs and clubs visited by the target market.

Not through supermarkets and traditional bars where Dad's beer is sold.

<u>Promotion</u>: A series of six ads representing the six brews/music styles. Ads to feature performers from that music genre singing about "their beer" being for them not their Dad. One song sung in six different styles.

Under-bottlecap sales promotion with instant prizes like free beer, CDs and baseball caps. Major prize for each brew/music would be an all expenses paid trip, anywhere in the world, to a live concert featuring the music of the brew. That is, a Rock concert for the Rock winner, a Pop concert for the Pop winner, etc.

The team came up with all this in less than 30 minutes.

Some Suggestions

Naturally these suggestions are in random order!

1. You might need to stop yourself from thinking this is silly. I admit it seems strange, but it works.
2. Don't reject the word you get if it seems too hard. Make yourself find the link.
3. Stop yourself from forcing a link to an idea you already have.
4. Don't create too many steps between the random word and your ideas. For example, Stereo leads to music, then The

Beatles, then Liverpool, then Strawberry Fields, then gardens, then roses, then florists, then Valentine's Day, then Christmas. *Oh, let's have a strawberry-flavoured Christmas beer.* That's far too many steps and completely unnecessary. Great ideas will come if you focus on the immediate features and benefits.

Variations on a Theme

There are many ways you can use randomness as your Light Bulb #2. Here are three ideas:

– Random Picture is a similar technique to Random Word. Randomly get a picture, for example, by opening a magazine to any page. Look carefully at the picture. Analyse it. What's going on and why? Then think of the colours, style and textures. List out your findings and then make the link back to Light Bulb #1.

– Random Racehorse: Pick up last Monday's newspaper and turn to the Sports section. Your stimulus will be the name of the racehorse that won the fourth race last weekend. Apply the same techniques as Random Word. (I bet you will get lots of winning ideas with this one.)

– Random Object is similar again, but this time you get to look at and hold the noun. That can help stimulate ideas.

Random Exercises

1. Go to the Random Words on the next page and find the B22 word. Write out the features and benefits of that word.

2. Find a link between those features and benefits and your most pressing problem. Note: there WILL be a link.

3. You know Random Word, Random Picture, Random Racehorse and Random Object. What other Random things or activities could be used to help you generate ideas?

4. I have suggested you choose tangible nouns as your Random Words. Do you think that you could also make Random Word work if you chose an adjective, like 'peaceful'?

5. Find the nearest green thing to where you are sitting. Now write down the features and benefits of it. Find some relationship between those features and benefits and your *ability to hold a conversation.*

Random Words

	A	B	C	D	E
1	Computer	Knife	Scissors	Air conditioner	Frog
2	Egg-beater	Forest	Tent	Cuckoo clock	Chocolate
3	Goldfish	Skyscraper	Prairie dog	Pillow	Garden
4	Rope	Hormones	Fruit cake	Cold cream	Garage
5	Beard	Comb	Sock	Hippopotamus	Husband
6	Toes	Toy	Soap	Curtains	Bowl
7	Telephone	Piano	Condom	Hamburger	Parking space
8	Floor	Map	Shark	Camp-fire	Jelly
9	Megaphone	Wire	Desert	Prawn	Ladder
10	Toothbrush	Diary	Pizza	VCR	Spotlight
11	Stamp	Snorkel	Earthquake	Eye drops	Chair
12	Bumblebee	Milk	Flag	Chess	Nose
13	Plan	CD	Coffin	Tennis racket	Elastic
14	Tissue-paper	Transsexual	Drapes	Beer	Waterbed
15	Pencil	Mouse	Shop	Perfume	Drip tray
16	Book	Rattle snake	In-tray	Baby food	Toaster
17	Band-aid	Baby	Bicycle pump	Gel	Corkscrew
18	Teacher	Swamp	Pineapple	Soup	Hand towel
19	Rainforest	Nurse	Wheel	Umpire	Transformer
20	Apartment	Rose	Airport	Fins	Pickle
21	Alligator	Drawer	Teapot	Worm	TNT
22	Needle	Cave	Coffee grinder	Policeman	Fuel tank
23	Pasta	Motor oil	Chap stick	Magazine	Aqualung
24	Calendar	Wig	Sweet potato	Vitamin C	Woman
25	Orange	Football	Lozenge	Floppy disk	Cashewnut
26	Brick	Church	Wedding ring	Button	Balloon
27	Rock	Tiger	Gear stick	Paper cup	Tie rack
28	Greeting card	Scarf	Camel	DVD	Boxing ring
29	Television	Pimple	Seaweed	Ice cream	Glue
30	Jacket	Ticket	Handbag	Door knob	Rug

7
Eyes of Experts

Q: How many consultants does it take to change a light bulb?

A: I'll have an estimate for you a week from Monday.

If you want to be *uncreative*, address your issues from your normal point of view. When you do that, your preconditioning and your prejudices will get in the way of your thinking. You will look for solutions that fit your mind, so all you'll come up with is the expected answer.

If you want to *flick your switch* try coming at the issue from a different person's point of view. When you do that you are using the other person as your Light Bulb #2.

You've probably used this tool before without knowing it. Remember when you were a child and you had a problem to face all alone? Maybe you asked yourself, *What would Mummy do?*

I'm not suggesting you use your Mummy to help you at work. I'm not suggesting you shouldn't either. But there are some people you should not choose as your Light Bulb #2. If you choose people from your own company, your boss, for example, you'll just be looking for the answer that fits his or her mind. Or if you're a consultant and you choose your client as your Light Bulb #2, you'll just come up with ideas your client would have thought of. So why did she need you? Using a person related to the issue as your second Light Bulb is just second-guessing. It's not creative. In fact, it's dangerous.

Whose Eyes?

So who do you choose? Well, it's not called Eyes of Experts for nothing. Choose Experts. But choose them from different industries from your own otherwise you'll just be copying a competitor. Choose people who were successful in achieving their goals. And choose people you know a lot about because you are going to try to put them in your place to see what they would do.

If you don't know how those Experts went about solving problems, how are you going to apply their thinking?

And what if you don't know anything about any Expert? Then put this book down and pick up some biographies of famous people and start reading. (Just don't forget to come back to this book after you've read the biographies.) Or if you can't wait to solve your problem, choose a different creative tool.

There are just four simple steps for this tool.

1. Identify the issue you are addressing. (Light Bulb #1.)
2. Choose three Experts from other fields (Light Bulb #2.)
3. Write down the modus operandi or methods of these experts in their own fields. If you're working in a team, discuss with other team members.
4. Now apply those methods to your issue.

An Expert Example

This example is taken from a workshop we conducted last year in Singapore. Here is a summary of the exercise.

1. The issue was: *How can we get the Singapore football team to reach the finals of the 2010 World Cup?*
2. The Experts they chose were Bill Gates, Singapore Senior Minister Lee Kwan Yew and Osama bin Laden.
3. Modus Operandi. After discussing each of the experts, they decided on these:
   Bill Gates
   • Extreme wealth; buys success
   • Computer expert
   • Almost monopoly control.

Lee Kwan Yew

- Unwavering determination
- Legislates for the greater good
- Builds businesses in line with government objectives.

Osama bin Laden

- Musters fanatical support
- Trains youngsters
- The element of surprise.

4. Next, they applied the modus operandi to the issue.

Light Bulb #1:
Singapore World
Cup finalists in
2010

Light Bulb #3:
New ideas

Light Bulb #2:
Eyes of Experts:
Bill Gates;
Lee Kwan Yew;
Osama bin Laden

Here is a summary of the outcomes, in no particular order. See if you can trace the ideas back to the Experts they came from.

-   Elevate the status of sports people in general and football players in particular so that parents encourage their children to play sport rather than just study.
-   Set up training camps for the young. Identify potential football stars at the youngest possible age and treat them like the elite athletes they will become. Send them to privileged schools and have them trained by the best coaches.

- Buy overseas players to play alongside Singapore's best. Don't wait until overseas players are over the hill. Bring them here while they are still in their prime.
- Nationalise all the football clubs and introduce strict guidelines on performance. Base funding on the results achieved.
- Organise international games against quality opposition at every age level from 10 onwards.
- Handsomely reward the members of every winning international team, regardless of age level.
- Create national heroes of successful football players.
- Build computer programs on football tactics so that young people can learn the theory of the game even before they can play it.
- Send players overseas to live and train in kinder climates.
- Subsidise businesses that include football holidays in their sales promotion prizes.
- Introduce football 'national service' for all boys aged between 10 and 12 to identify future stars.
- Make sport a school subject that carries equal weight as Second Language or Science.
- Build air-conditioned football grounds in each neighborhood so that the hot, humid weather doesn't stop players from training.

- Create a football training hub in Singapore to turn the training of elite football players into a self funding business.

- Take all potential 2010 players of the 2006 World Cup to experience the atmosphere of the event.

- Write a national song about football and have it recorded by the most popular Singapore singers. Promote it on radio and television. Teach it in schools.

- Scout the world, especially Brazil, Argentina and Cameroon for youngsters with the most potential. Bring them and their families to Singapore, give them citizenship and a standard of living they could never hope to achieve in their homeland.

- Buy a Premiere League team in England and study success from the inside. Include in every player's contract a condition that they spend one week in Singapore every year conducting coaching clinics.

Not bad, huh? If the Football Association of Singapore and the government implemented these, Singaporeans might want to book their 2010 Wold Cup tickets now.

Some Expert Tips

If you're using this tool with a team, let the team members choose the Experts. And don't censor the choice of the Expert on the grounds of policies, politics or morals. I have seen good ideas emerge from Experts as diverse as Adolf Hitler, Madonna, Oprah Winfrey, Alexander the Great and Richard Branson.

If you're working in a team, don't be concerned if only one person knows how the Expert operates. Get that person to explain to the group and have him/her identify the three or four operating methods that you could apply to your problem.

As usual, write down every idea that comes up, no matter how practical or sensible. Reserve judgment for another time.

By the way, you can use this tool by yourself as long as you have enough knowledge of Experts to draw upon.

Industrial Roundabout

There's a variation on the Eyes of Experts tools that is easy to learn and use. It's called Industrial Roundabout. Instead of using the Eyes of Expert people, you use the expertise of other industries to come up with creative ideas for your own.

For example, if you are in the under-garments industry, you will naturally be drawn to solutions already used in your industry. Your tendency will be to develop incremental ideas – those that build on the past. If you were to use another industry as your second Light Bulb you may well find new ways to address your issue.

Assume you are marketing a new bra for the "first bra" market. Instead of looking to the under-garment industry for ideas, why not apply the Industrial Roundabout tool and look at it from the point of view of some other industry. Let's follow the thinking through, using the same steps as Eyes of Experts.

1. The issue: *How do we market a new bra to the pre-teen "first bra" market?*

2. You can choose as many different industries as you want. Three is a good number. For this example we'll use just one: the cosmetics industry.

3. Modus operandi of the cosmetics industry.
   The overarching modus operandi is creating long-term loyalty via a number of ways, for example:
   • Attracting new customers with low-priced entry products
   • Offering gifts with purchase (GWP), or lower priced purchase with purchase (PWP)
   • Positioning themselves as skin experts
   • Having a trained and dedicated sales force
   • Providing free Club memberships that bring news, advice and special offers
   • Sweepstakes with interesting prizes
   • Helping customers change their look through make-overs

4. Now we apply the modus operandi of the cosmetics industry to the issue and generate ideas.

Light Bulb #1:
A new "first bra" for pre-teens

Light Bulb #2:
Industrial Roundabout: How the cosmetics industry markets its products

Light Bulb #3:
New marketing ideas

Here is a sample of ideas that may come from forcing these two Light Bulbs together. Create loyalty by:

– Marketing the first bra as a loss leader to get pre-teens into the brand.

– Offering GWP and/or PWP. Gift could be a washing bag for the bra or something else pre-teen girls are interested in, like cosmetics, magazine subscriptions, music, etc. PWP might be a special offer on other under-garments.

– Making 2-for-1 offers or packages of matching under-garments.

– Entering every purchase into a sweepstakes contest. Winners receive a full wardrobe from a famous teen fashion brand.

– Taking the Expert position and provide literature with advice on choosing a bra, fitting, washing care.

– Training the sales-people in expert fitting. Provide badges or other notices indicating fitting accreditation.

– Making buyers automatic members of a fashion club, accessed via the internet. The club would treat them as young adults not as kids. It would reward loyalty, provide up to date tips on grooming, dressing, fashion, underwear, music and other items of interest to pre-teens.

– Alternatively, tie in with an existing website that reaches the target market and take a prominent role. Go beyond simple web advertising.

These are just a few ideas generated using Industrial Roundabout. When you try it, use three industries, generate lots of ideas without censoring them. Then come back later and further develop the more promising ideas.

Try Your Expertise on These

1. List the Experts you think you know enough about to use with this tool. How many do you have?

2. Which famous people come to mind when you think of the following categories? Golf, Airlines, Government, Advertising, Telecommunications, Space Travel, TV Talk Shows, Basketball, Swimming, Music, Movies? Do you know enough about how these people became successful and how they go about their business?

3. Why might Bill Clinton be a poor Expert to use when thinking about more creative approaches to government in South Korea?

4. What are some of the issues you face that could be addressed with the Eyes of Experts tool?

8
What's Hot?

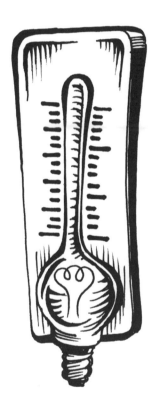

Q: How many teenage girls does it take to screw in a light bulb?

A: One, but she'll be on the phone for five hours telling all her friends about it.

Our third tool is called "What's Hot?" Like, what's interesting, motivating and going to grab attention?

To get started, let's think about the music industry and pop music in particular. Why is it so popular, besides the fact that millions of dollars are spent marketing the music and the singers? I think one of the reasons is because it connects with young people. The songs are about the sorts of things that are on young people's minds: *love, broken hearts, confusion, fashion, getting noticed, hopes, fears, being yourself, and so on.*

The pop stars don't create these interests in young people. They tap into something that's already there. But no matter how cool the videos and marketing, how successfully would Britney Spears connect with young people if she sang about the Nasdaq, life insurance, care for ageing parents or gardening suggestions?

The question for us is, *"How can we use the same sort of approach to connect with people and market our products and services in a creative way. (Without necessarily singing to them.)"*

And the answer starts with figuring out what is already in someone's mind and attaching our product or service to it.

Remember William James? He figured this out 100 years ago. He said, when talking about getting new things in people's minds… *"our conscious effort should not be so much to impress and retain (information) as to connect it with something else already there."*

The Hot Steps

Let's say we want to develop an idea to sell more of our product. Maybe we're looking for an advertising or sales promotion idea. What's Hot? will be our Light Bulb #2.

These are the steps involved:

1. Decide who we are trying to reach... in other words, our Target Market.

2. Figure out What's Interesting for the target market. Generate a list of all the things that interest them, including the trends they are influenced by. It helps to *think* like the target market. Try to get at least 25 things.

3. Now, we Cross Off everything on the list that is related to our product area. The reason we take off related things is because they are in the same 'filing cabinet drawer' as our product, so they are obvious links. And we are trying to do something less expected.

4. From what is left on the list, we decide What's Hot? They will be the things that are extremely interesting or new interests. Identify things that are aspirational or motivational. Especially identify things that the target market obsesses over or dreams of owning.

5. Ask the Magic Question: *How can I use this?* And come up with new ideas by connecting the Hot things to the product or service you are marketing.

A Red Hot Example

Assume we are the marketers of *premium home entertainment systems*. Like those giant, flatscreen TVs with house-shaking surround sound, DVD, video and even Internet. (Drool, drool.) The sort that costs around $20,000. Let's follow the example through the five steps:

1. <u>Target Market</u>: *Affluent middle-aged family men who want to enjoy their ultimate entertainment dream – larger than life sports and movies – from the comfort of their favourite chair.*

2. <u>What's Interesting?</u>: Here's a sample of what's interesting to these men:

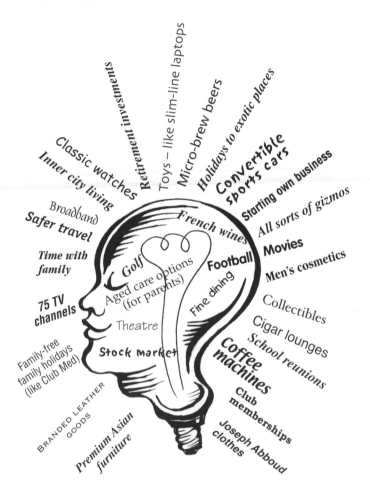

(That's enough for now)

3. <u>Cross Off</u>: Now we shorten the list. We delete anything that is closely related to our product, like movies, spectator sports, stock market, because they are naturally associated with home entertainment systems.

4. <u>What's Hot?</u> Now we choose the hottest items. For the exercise, let's just focus on one thing: *convertible sports cars (hot red, of course)*. In reality, we'd do this for several of the Hot items and then decide which ones to go with.

5. <u>Ask the Magic Question</u>: *How can I use men's interest in convertible sports cars to market our home entertainment systems?*

Now we force the link. We use Porsche as the convertible sports car in his mind and see what ideas we can generate for the Marketing 4 Ps:

Light Bulb #1:
Home
Entertainment
System

Light Bulb #3:
New marketing
ideas

Light Bulb #2:
What's Hot?
Porsche
convertible

Product:

- Design the product to look more like a Porsche. For example, make the fascia of the TV or stereo look like the dashboard of a Porsche. Make the exterior lines resemble the profile of a Porsche. Base the colour options on the Porsche colours. Make the remote control more sporty in shape.
- Go further... get Porsche to design the home entertainment system.
- Co-brand the product with Porsche Design.
- Make an in-car unit that matches the Porsche interior.
- Make a special "listening chair", designed like a Porsche seat and sell it with the system.
- Name the home entertainment system "Convertible" because it converts from TV to DVD to video to Internet in an instant.
- Offer after-sales service like you get with a new car. Log books, regular servicing, extended warranty, etc.

Price:

- It's a premium product, associated with premium sports cars. Therefore the price has to be premium.
- Like a Porsche, offer cash sale, hire purchase, leasing, rental, trade-ins.

Promotion:

- Use visual images of Porsches on the TV screen in our print and point of purchase advertising. It will get the target's attention.

- Go further... set the TV ad around a Porsche-driving man. Ideas like these come to mind:
  - He loves his entertainment system so much he has converted the garage into a home theatre, leaving the sports car out in the rain.
  - The TV screen is so big that he sits in his convertible to watch it – as if he's at the drive-in theatre.
  - He drives home at race-track speed just so he can spend more time in front of the home entertainment system.
  - We see him, as if he's driving a convertible... wind in the hair, fantastic scenery like the Riviera whizzing by, we hear the sounds of the racing engine. We pull back to see he's in his living room. The scenery is on the TV and the sound is coming from the speakers. The wind in his hair is just a fan blowing in his living room.
  - Use a famous Porsche convertible-driving celebrity as spokesperson for the brand.
- We can offer "test drives" of the home entertainment system. Place it in the customer's home for a week so he can test it and fall in love with it.
- Joint promotion with Porsche - three ideas
  - A Porsche for a day when he buys our product.
  - Offer the chance to win our product when he test drives a Porsche.
  - A free home entertainment system when he buys a Porsche.
    These ideas cost us little but associate our brand with Porsche.

Place:

– We can put a Porsche at the retail outlet to draw attention to the product and the promotion.
– We can set up a sales boutique at the Porsche dealership.

Imagine how many ideas we could come up with if we pursued some of the other Hot items in his life. Like French wines, Club Med or Golf.

A Hotbed of Ideas

You can use What's Hot? by yourself or in a small team. If you have a large team, facilitate stages 1, 2 and 3 then divide up into smaller teams. Allocate a Hot item for each small team and give them about 30 minutes to come up with ideas. Then get everyone back together and compare ideas. Adopt the best ideas.

What's Hot? is especially useful when you're looking for an advertising or sales promotion idea. It's quick and easy and will always give you a result. Just as important… people like using this tool. Try it.

The Heat Is On

Now let's turn up the heat with these challenging questions.

1. Consider teenage girls and make-up.
   - What are 25 things that interest them – besides teenage boys?
   - Cut your list of 25 interesting things by removing anything to do with make-up.
   - Now choose the three hottest things. These are the ones that grab attention or motivate teenage girls.
   - Now generate at least three sales promotion ideas to launch a new brand of make-up.

2. If you were marketing a PDA, who would be your core target market? Be specific. ("Anyone with hands" is too broad.)
   - For your PDA target market, what is interesting? Now What's Hot? Don't forget to delete anything that is naturally related to PDAs.
   - Choose one of your Hot items and force links between it and the PDA. Come up with at least 10 ideas.

9
Curly Questions

Q: How many philosophers does it take to change a light bulb?

A: Hmmm... well that's an interesting question isn't it?

When I was a kid I used to ask my older brother, Robert, lots of questions. Here's a typical exchange between a 5-year-old (me) and a 15-year-old (him).

> Me : "Why do they call it a shovel?"
> Him : "Why do they call you Wayne?"
> Me : "Because that's my name."
> Him : "That's why they call it a shovel... because that's its name."
> Me : "But that's not right!"
> Him : "Ask a silly question, get a silly answer."

Now I never thought my questions were silly, but it does raise an interesting thought. Whether I am asking a question of others or of myself, if I ask a silly question, maybe I'll get a silly answer. If I ask a serious question, maybe I'll get a serious answer. If I ask a predictable question, maybe I'll get a predictable answer. *And if I ask a creative question, maybe I can get a creative answer.*

With this tool the Curly Question (or creative question) is your Light Bulb #2. By Curly, I don't mean difficult. I mean different, thought provoking and unexpected. Perhaps even completely off-the-wall.

A Curly Example

Let's start with a simple example of a Curly Question. Actually it's only slightly curly (wavy?) because you have probably heard it before. But let's work through it before introducing more complex Curly Questions.

If your brand were a car, what sort of car would it be and why?

Light Bulb #1:
Your Brand

Light Bulb #2:
Curly Question:
If your brand were
a car, what sort of
car would it be
and why?

Light Bulb #3:
New
understanding
of your brand

This sort of question gets the mind thinking about the brand in a different way. It forces a link between what you know about the brand and what you know about cars. It brings answers like this one which came up in a workshop I facilitated recently with a worldwide communications company:

> *"If our brand were a car, we'd be a blue Mitsubishi Lancer. We'd be blue because we're a bit different from the common silver or white but we're not bold enough to be red."* They went on...

> *"A Lancer is an inoffensive car. It doesn't hurt or shock anyone. It doesn't go particularly fast. We're like that. Inoffensive, even bland. But we like to pretend we are fast-paced so our car would have GT stripes to make it look like it goes fast. We'd probably have a nodding dog on the back*

window ledge because we're friendly. Of course we'd rather be a BMW but we're not successful enough."

They went on from there to figure out exactly what their brand stood for. They were able to identify the areas that needed fixing and the areas that were performing satisfactorily. The discussion brought a healthy dose of the truth and the participants had fun with the metaphor.

By the way, if you don't want to think of your brand or company as a car, (maybe yours *is* a car brand), try a different question. Like, if your brand were a TV show, which one would it be and why? That should get the discussion going.

The Flintstones

That's what we did in a workshop in Australia when middle-management met to talk about their company's future. The company, they decided, was like the Flintstones. Middle-management felt the company had hit bedrock. When we delved more deeply into it we found out why.

According to the middle-managers, the directors were a bit like Fred Flintstone: big-talking, proud, not too bright, demanding, unfocused, sometimes bullying, and living in the past. They even joked that, like Fred, the managing director wore the same clothes every day.

Middle-management thought they were like Wilma: long-suffering, steady and predictable. They believed they constantly covered for Fred's mistakes and strange behaviours.

There was a Dino equivalent. A young man who ran around madly making lots of noise and getting Fred's attention without actually achieving anything. And to complete the family, they even identified one of the younger staff as Pebbles: the attractive young woman who could get senior management to do whatever she wanted. (Don't ask.)

After they had some fun with this, the managers started to notice some other similarities. Their systems were so old they needed carbon dating. They were still doing things the way they had done them for years, even though the reasons for those systems had long since gone. To their credit, the Wilmas admitted outdated systems were as much their fault as Fred's.

The company's technology was also in the stone age. This made everyone's lives more stressful than necessary as they struggled to meet the increasing demands of their customers.

After they had exhausted their Flintstones story, we turned their attention to the future. They decided they needed to become more like the Jetsons. The session then turned into a positive discussion of future possibilities. They developed a vision for a future company with a co-operative management, and with energy- and stress-saving technologies and systems.

We presented the ideas to the Directors, carefully disguising some of the Fred analogies, and one year later things are changing for the better. The Directors still occasionally behave a bit like Fred, but they're getting better. They're more open to middle-management's suggestions. The technology is being updated and old systems are being replaced with more efficient ones. The work environment is being overhauled. There's a new buzz about the place.

Dino has been neutered and Pebbles has moved on.

That's the value of applying a Curly Question. Lots of involvement, fun and the truth spoken without fear.

Now let's set up some situations and some appropriate Curly Questions. Once you've seen some examples you'll be able to make up your own questions. I have listed here 10 issues you might want to explore at work. Separately I have listed 10 Curly Questions you could ask yourself or your team. See if you can figure out which Curly Question best addresses each issue.

Sample Issues

1. Review your company policies and procedures.

2. Recognise your company's real successes and failures.

3. Figure out what clients think you need to improve.

4. Determine what staff think of management's style.

5. Identify where you or your staff lack skills.

6. Improve your department's performance.

7. Figure out where your brand is most vulnerable.

8. Assess how well you are performing in your job.

9. Understand the current mood, fears and hopes of the staff.

10. Uncover who or what is stopping your company from being more successful.

Sample Curly Questions

A. Think about being a child and all the things you had to do that didn't make sense to you. What do we do at work that's like that?

B. If the managing director called an emergency all-staff meeting this afternoon, what do you think it might be about?

C. Imagine you are our biggest competitor. How might you plan to destroy our brand?

D. If someone from outer-space visited our company, what would it find most strange?

E. If our work team were a sports team (football, basketball, etc) tell us about the game we just lost. Why did we lose? What skills let us down? What can we learn from the game to take into next week's match?

F. What if our company died tomorrow and you had to write the obituary. What would you write?

G: If our fairy godmother were to wave her wand over us and turn us instantly into an incredibly successful and cohesive unit, what new skills or behaviours would we have?

H. Suppose you were to swap jobs with your key customer. What changes would each of you make to your new workplace?

I. What has our competitor done in the last 12 months that we wished we had done first? Why didn't we do it?

J. Imagine you were poached by a competitor. What particular skills would they be expecting you to bring to their company? Now imagine you were fired from your current company. What would have been the most likely reasons?

How did you make out? Were you able to match them up? Check your match up with my suggestions on page 151.

Five Ways to Write Curly Questions

You don't necessarily need to write your own Curly Questions. You can adapt mine to cover your own situation. But if you want to try writing your own, that's great. You don't need to be Einstein to do it. Here's how.

Start with a direct question just to clarify in your own mind what you are trying to achieve. For example:

How effective are our policies and procedures?

Then look for a Curly way to ask the question using one of these five general approaches:

1. Analogies
2. Speculation
3. Role Reversal
4. Imagination
5. Reflection

Here's a note on each approach and an example of the technique in use, showing how each can lead to a different Curly Question to address the same issue.

Analogies: Look for an opportunity to liken your situation to something your audience already understands. Try sport, marriage, music, school, movies or food. Well, maybe not marriage. Nobody understands that.

- Straight Question: *How effective are our policies and procedures?*
- Curly Question (using the Analogy of childhood): *Think about being a child and all the things you had to do that didn't make sense to you. What do we do at work that's like that?*

Speculation: These are "What if" questions. To make them work, you think of an unusual situation and ask your audience what would happen if this unusual situation were to arise.

- Straight Question: *How effective are our policies and procedures?*
- Curly Question (using Speculation): *What if we closed this company and started an entirely new company tomorrow. What policies and procedures would we keep from the old company and which ones would we throw away?*

Role Reversal: These Curly Questions aim at getting the view of someone we would not normally consult, like a customer, competitor or a supplier. Participants like these questions because their answers can be ascribed to someone else. People are less fearful of voicing their opinion.

- Straight Question: *How effective are our policies and procedures?*
- Curly Question (using Role Reversal): *Imagine you are our biggest customer. What does our company do that you, as a customer, really love? That you really hate?*

Imagination: This approach takes us into a completely unreal world, like the world of magic, fairies or wizards. It is another good technique to use when you want to get to the truth without putting the participants under pressure.

- Straight Question: *How effective are our policies and procedures?*
- Curly Question (using Imagination): *If a powerful wizard cast a spell on us to rid us of ineffective policies and practices, which ones would magically disappear and why?*

Reflection: Look for an opportunity to reflect on the past and ask an interesting question that encourages people to find real examples of action or inaction that shed light on the issue.

- Straight Question: *How effective are our policies and procedures?*
- Curly Question (using Reflection): *What opportunities were lost in the last year because of our ways of doing business internally, with suppliers or with customers?*

When to Use Them

Curly Questions are great for group sessions. So use this tool when you want to involve the team. Or when you think others might have a better understanding of the issues you face.

Curly Questions get everyone involved because the questions aren't as direct or threatening as the ones we are used to facing. They are also more fun and that encourages open dialogue and creativity. Don't worry if the discussion goes down the wrong track because eventually it will get to the heart of the issue.

1. What issues might these Curly Questions help you with?
   - If all of the management team retired at once, what would happen to our company?
   - My crystal ball says that in five years our department (or company, or brand) wins an award for the best in its class. What changes did we make between now and then that got us that award?
   - If we came up with a sensational idea, who or what would prevent it from being adopted?
   - What unspoken or undocumented 'rules' exist in the office and how do they affect business?

2. What Curly Questions can you come up with to help you with these issues?
   - Understand the pressures faced by members of your team and how those pressures affect them.
   - Discover why so much time is wasted in your organisation.
   - Figure out why your company is unable to attract the best talent in the industry.
   - Determine what you can do to improve creativity in your department.

10
Extremes

Q: How many extremists does it take to change a light bulb?

A: Six. One to change the bulb, and five to take the credit when it explodes.

I have included this tool for those who are looking for ways to capture attention and create some memorable communication about a product or service. For example, through an advertisement.

There are two ways of using Extremes: the positive way and the negative way. To distinguish them from each other, let's call the Positive Extreme EXAGGERATION and the Negative Extreme DEPRIVATION.

Exaggeration

Imagine you want to promote a product and you're looking for a creative way to draw attention to its benefit. But when you analyse the product you find the benefit is rather small or unimportant. What you need to do is Exaggerate the benefits. In doing so you can make a small benefit get noticed and the communication more memorable.

There is only one rule you need to remember:

Because you are exaggerating the benefit you can't make the ad look too real. You have to introduce Extreme drama or Extreme humour in order to ensure the viewer or the reader is not tricked into believing something that isn't true. By exaggerating *everything* in the ad you will avoid being accused of false or misleading advertising.

Here's how to get started:

1. **The Brief:** Identify the core target market for the product. Interrogate the features of the product and figure out the key benefit of those features. The benefit must be something the target market wants. Make sure you focus on only one benefit. Essentially, this is the BRIEF. (In reality

it is much more complicated, but this is enough for us to examine the approach.)

2. **The Proposition:** Cut through all the detail in the Brief and determine the one thing what you want the target market to believe about the brand. This is your PROPOSITION.

3. **The Idea:** Let your mind go and exaggerate the Proposition. But keep it general. Don't go into details. This is your IDEA.

4. **The Execution:** If you have a sound Idea there will be many ways to create an ad. What actually happens in the ad is called the EXECUTION.

Three Examples

Example #1: Tip Top Bread (M&C Saatchi Sydney, Australia)

1. **The Brief:** *Mothers want their growing children to eat healthy bread, while kids want to eat white bread. Tip Top bread satisfies kids, because it's white, and mothers because it's healthy. One sandwich provides one third of kids' daily iron needs and the iron makes them strong.*

2. **The Proposition:** *Makes you strong.*

3. **The Idea:** (Exaggerate strong) *How strong? Dangerously strong; Super strong.* (This gives us plenty of latitude to execute the idea.)

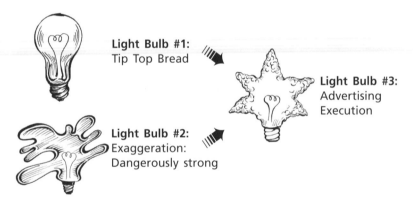

Light Bulb #1: Tip Top Bread

Light Bulb #2: Exaggeration: Dangerously strong

Light Bulb #3: Advertising Execution

4. **The Execution:** This Idea could be executed in several ways. For example, a boy turns into Superman by eating Tip Top bread. Or he fights The Rock for the WWE title. M&C Saatchi's approach produced this wonderful ad. In a nutshell:

   A teenage boy wakes up and goes about his morning routine, but he is so strong from eating Tip Top bread that he accidentally smashes everything he touches.

Open on a scene where a school boy wakes to the sound of his alarm clock.

The ringing alarm clock is slammed through the dresser by the sleepy boy.

He walks across his room, reaches to open the door, but the door knob crumbles in his hand.

The boy opens the sliding shower door, but it flies off the rails and slams into a wall outside the bathroom.

While dressing himself and adjusting his tie, he rips it into two pieces.

The boy walks into the kitchen where his mum is making sandwiches.

V/O: The White Stuff from Tip Top with iron fibre plus.

Boy in a deep voice: "I might just have one sandwich today thanks Mum."

V/O: One sandwich contains at least one third of the recommended daily iron intake.

V.O: It's powerful stuff.

Reproduced by permission of M&C Saatchi, Sydney and TipTop, GeorgeWeston Foods Baking Division.

Example #2: Rute 180 Discount Clothing Store
(Leo Burnett, Copenhagen)

1. **The Brief:** *Rute 180 is a discount store that sells branded products at discount prices. Their Mega Sale prices are even lower than usual.*
2. **The Proposition:** *Cheaper than cheap.*
3. **The Idea:** *How cheap? So cheap they're "throw-away" cheap.*
   (This is non-specific and therefore gives us plenty of latitude to execute the idea.)

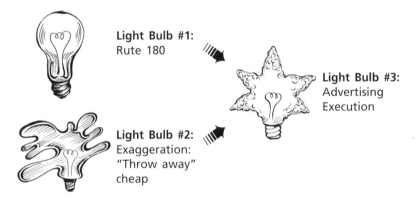

Light Bulb #1:
Rute 180

Light Bulb #3:
Advertising
Execution

Light Bulb #2:
Exaggeration:
"Throw away"
cheap

4. **The Execution:** Leo Burnett Copenhagen did it in two very unusual ways:
   (i) *A woman, resting after shopping at Rute 180 Discount Store, is annoyed by a barking dog. Rather than move, she distracts the dog by throwing a brand new Nike shoe to him.*
   (ii) *A man with a cold is waiting for a train. He needs to blow his nose but has no tissue or handkerchief. So he blows his nose on a brand new Diesel shirt.*

Sound effects throughout: Street noises and the loud incessant yelping of a large dog.

Open on a street scene where we see a woman sitting at a sidewalk café. On the chair next to her we see a bag from Rute 180 Discount Store.

She's trying to enjoy a relaxing cup of coffee following her shopping trip but is distracted by the continuous barking and yelping of a dog that is tied up near her.

We can tell by the look on her face that she's not enjoying this. Finally, she reaches into her shopping bag and takes out a brand new Nike sports shoe.

She stands and throws the shoe down, next to the dog.

The dog stops barking immediately as it picks up the shoe in its mouth and "fights" it.

We cut to black and see a super that says:

Nike Airmax Tailwinds are only Dkr 499 anyway.

Cut to Rute 180 logo and the title:

THE MEGA SALE
JUNE 29 – JULY 12

Reproduced by permission of Leo Burnett, Copenhagen, Denmark and Rute 180.

Sound effects throughout: Busy railway station with sound of trains coming and going.

Open on a railway platform as a train departs the station. There is a man standing on the platform. He is holding a shopping bag from Rute 180 Discount Store.

He seems to have a cold. We see him wipe his nose with his hand.

As the camera moves in, we see him open the shopping bag and take out a T-shirt he has just bought. We know the shirt is new because we can see the label is still attached to it.

He takes the shirt and blows his nose on it a few times.

Then he walks to the rubbish bin on the railway platform and throws the shirt away.

We cut to black and see a super that says:

DIESEL T-shirt is only Dkr 99 anyway.

Cut to Rute 180 logo and the title:

THE MEGA SALE
JUNE 29 – JULY 12

Reproduced by permission of Leo Burnett, Copenhagen, Denmark and Rute 180.

Example #3: Campaign Brief Asia
(Saatchi & Saatchi, Hong Kong)

1. **The Brief:** *Campaign Brief is an advertising industry magazine with its focus on creativity. While other industry magazines report what is happening in the entire industry, Campaign Brief reports purely from a creative point of view. Campaign Brief wants to own the position of the industry authority on creativity and ideas.*

2. **The Proposition:** *Reporting all the biggest ideas.*

3. **The Idea:** (Exaggerate biggest ideas) *Enormous ideas; earth-shattering ideas; mind-blowing ideas... killer ideas.*

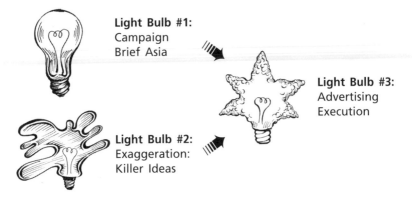

Light Bulb #1: Campaign Brief Asia

Light Bulb #2: Exaggeration: Killer Ideas

Light Bulb #3: Advertising Execution

4. **The Execution:** Saatchi & Saatchi developed a multi-award winning campaign of three print ads based on this idea.

   Using the metaphor of the light bulb for an idea, show how a reader of Campaign Brief is killed by a gigantic idea she/ he reads about.

Reproduced by permission of Saatchi & Saatchi, Hong Kong and Campaign Brief Asia.

Deprivation

The other way of using Extremes is Deprivation. We take the benefit away and then we see how that deprivation affects people.

This is a particularly powerful tool when you are advertising something that people take for granted, like a good night's sleep, milk, water or television. Or something they would prefer not to think about.

Taking the benefit away is a negative approach. Clients often worry about negative advertising. Don't be concerned. It is far better to advertise the negative in a powerful way than to advertise the positive in a weak way. Besides, if you have a product that people take for granted, they won't be interested in being reminded of its benefits. The negative ad will work if you leave people with a positive view of your brand.

As with Exaggeration, you can make the Deprivation communication work harder through Extreme drama or Extreme humour. Using the Deprivation approach is quite straight forward:

1.   **The Brief:** As with Exaggeration, identify the core target market for the product. Interrogate the features of the product and figure out the key benefit of those features. The benefit must be something the target market wants. Make sure you focus on only one benefit. (Again, it's more complicated, but this will do for our purposes.)

2.   **The Proposition:** Cut through all the detail and determine what you want the target market to believe about the brand.

3.   **The Idea:** Now imagine what a day, a family, a business or a life would be like without that benefit. Let

your mind go and think of all the consequences of depriving the target market of the benefit. But keep it general. Don't get specific at this stage.

4.   **The Execution:** There will be many ways to execute a good Idea.

Two More Examples

Example 1: Ego Pension Fund (Leo Burnett, Warsaw, Poland)

1.   **The Brief:** *Ego Pension Fund has a strong record of building pension nest eggs. Regular contributions to the Fund will ensure that investors continue to enjoy their lifestyle after they retire.*

     (People in their 20s, 30s and 40s, don't want to think about retirement. To get their attention we have to do something different. Hence a Deprivation strategy.)

2.   **The Proposition:** *Continue to enjoy life after retirement.*

3.   **The Idea:** (Use Deprivation) *Show the terrible life you might have to live after retirement if you <u>don't</u> invest in Ego Pension Fund.*

 Light Bulb #1: Ego Pension Fund

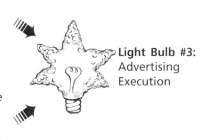 **Light Bulb #3:** Advertising Execution

 Light Bulb #2: Deprivation: The terrible life you might have if you don't invest in Ego

4. **The Execution:** There are many ways to execute the idea. For example, show a previously successful businessman begging on the street. Or a man at his retirement party, handing back the keys to his luxury company car and being given a bicycle as his retirement gift.

   Leo Burnett Warsaw chose to use humour and did it sensationally with these two Executions:

   (i) A retired man and his wife have to <u>simulate</u> a skiing holiday at home because they can't afford the real thing.

   (ii) This time a retired man and his wife <u>simulate</u> a boating holiday at home because they can't afford the real thing.

Soundtrack: Swiss Alps yodeling music throughout.

Wearing a woolly scarf and hat, an elderly chap bounces on an armchair in his living room, desperately clutching a pair of skis.

Concentrating hard, he mimics an alpine decent while a flurry of snow blows into his face.

Trouble is, it's not snow.

The camera cuts to his long suffering missus, wearily plucking a dead chicken besides an electric fan.

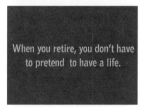

Cut to black and super:

When you retire, you don't have to pretend to have a life.

Cut to logo:

Ego Pension Fund.

Reproduced by permission of Leo Burnett, Warsaw, Poland and Ego Pension Fund.

Soundtrack: upbeat tropical holiday music throughout.

Unable to afford his own sailboat, a hapless pensioner resorts to a converted bathtub on his living room floor.

Replete with a captain's hat and tropical cocktail, he scans the horizon with his telescope.

He spots a scantily clad woman stranded on a desert island.

It's actually his wife, sitting on some cushions in the hallway, waving to him.

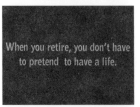

Cut to black and super:

When you retire, you don't have to pretend to have a life.

Cut to logo:

Ego Pension Fund.

Reproduced by permission of Leo Burnett, Warsaw, Poland and Ego Pension Fund.

When to Use Them

Extremes, whether Exaggeration or Deprivation, can lead to excellent TV commercials. They also work for print and other advertising media. Use them when the product benefit seems small or unexciting, or when advertising a low interest product.

They work particularly well together. That is, Deprive someone of the benefits of a product, then Exaggerate the effects of Deprivation. They both work better when the tone of the ad is Extreme humour or Extreme drama.

Next time you see an ad you really like, ask yourself whether the advertising agency used Extremes. Chances are they have.

Other Uses for Extremes

Advertising is not the only use for the Extremes approach. You can use Extreme thinking to come up with ideas for new products or new systems. Or to review what you already have in place.

For products, all you do is think through the benefits of the product and take it to its Extreme. What are the possibilities? What could it do? What could it look like?

Working systems and procedures are a bit like prescription drugs. They are used to solve particular problems, but they invariably have side effects. You can use Extreme Deprivation to help you think this through. Consider what would happen if you took the system away. If nothing bad would happen, streamline your procedures by removing the system. If there are negative consequences, consider whether you'd be better off by removing the system altogether and using other methods to overcome the negative effects. Of course, you can always stick with what you have, but only when there's good reason to do so.

Extreme Exercises

1. Make a list of 10 low-interest product categories. Recall the advertising for these products. Are the ads good? Are Exaggeration and Deprivation strategies being used?

2. Tape five ads from the TV and analyse them. Work out the Proposition (what the advertiser wants you to believe about the brand). Then identify the Idea (the creative way the Proposition is being used. Be careful not to describe the ad.) Then describe the Execution (what actually happens in the ad).

3. Complete these sentences using Exaggeration to create Ideas. (Keep it general and don't describe the Execution.)
    (i)   A tasty pasta sauce: *So tasty that...*
    (ii) An irresistible ice-cream: *So irresistible that...*
    (iii) A time-saving software: *Saves so much time that...*

4. Turn these Ideas into advertising Executions. Go on, *flick your creative switch.*
    (i)   Prices so low you'll be tempted to buy more than you need.
    (ii) A bed so comfortable we can't be held responsible for the consequences.
    (iii) A video camera so light you'll have to hold it down.

5. What might be the Exaggerated consequences if you:
    (i)   Deprive people of fresh water.
          (Advertising for the Water Board.)
    (ii) Deprive a traveling businesswoman of a good night's sleep. (Advertising for a 5-star hotel.)
    (iii) Deprive a businessman of International Roaming on his cell-phone. (Advertising for a telecom company.)

    Let your hair down. Make them Extreme.

11
Exquisite Corpse

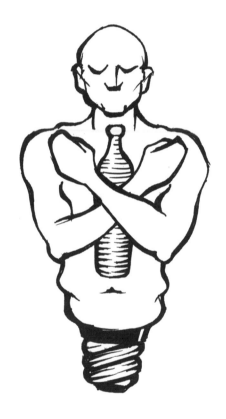

Q: How many Surrealists does it take to change a light bulb?

A: Two. One to hold the giraffe and the other to fill the bathtub with brightly coloured machine tools.

Surrealist art seems so strange you could be forgiven for wondering what it all means. Like many things, it makes a lot more sense when you understand the idea behind it.

I don't intend to explain the meaning of Surrealist Art here – even if I understood it – but it will be helpful to understand how the Surrealists got their ideas. One of the ways was called Exquisite Corpse, for reasons that will soon become dead obvious.

We're in Paris and it's 1925. There's a group of Surrealists, including André Breton, poet Jacques Prevert, painter Yves Tanguy and Marcel Duhamel the owner of the house at 54 rue de Chateau. They are having dinner and discussing the world. Breton describes the events that took place.

"When the conversation started to lose its interest in the facts and topics of the day...we used to pass to some game – written games in the beginning – combined in such a way that the elements of speech came face to face in the most paradoxical manner, and human communication, derailed from the beginning, set the mind running with the maximum of adventure."

– André Breton

Breton's wife added:

"Violent surprises prompted admiration, laughter, and stirred an unquenchable craving for new images – images inconceivable to one brain alone – born from the involuntary, unconscious, and unpredictable mixing of three or four heterogeneous minds."

– Simone Collinet

This is one of the games they played: Each person present secretly thought of a word. One thought of an adjective, another a noun, another a verb, another an adjective and the last person, another noun. Together they used their words to form the first sentence of its type, "le cadavre exquis boira le vin nouveau". Or, *the exquisite corpse will drink the new wine.*

Obviously that's where the name for this technique came from.

Sentences such as this conjured up strange visual images. And those images are what the Surrealists painted. The pictures were born from the *"unpredictable mixing of three or four heterogeneous minds"*.

Art or Business?

This might all be very well for art, but how can we use this idea in business?

The first thing to remember is something we have already discussed: that the creative mind can make anything work. We can find the connection if we look for it. There WILL be a way to use Exquisite Corpse to help you come up with more creative solutions to business problems, if you believe in it and apply sufficient brainpower.

An Exquisite Corpse sentence we create is just another example of the stimulus that helps us generate original ideas. It is Light Bulb #2. When we use a sentence generated in this way, we give ourselves a new place to focus our attention. And because the sentence is completely unrelated to the issue we are addressing, we will come at that issue from an entirely new direction.

Let's try it...

Imagine we face a business problem. Imagine we gather five or six people to brainstorm ideas. Let's say the problem we face is about being more creative in our business. We can define the challenge as *"How can we become more creative in everything we do?"*

Light Bulb #1: Our business as it stands now and everything we know about it, including our desire to make it more creative.

If we approach the problem in the usual way, we will be dwelling on the problem itself and creative ideas will be hard to come by.

But, if we start our team meeting with a quick game of Exquisite Corpse, we will come to our problem from a different angle. We will free our minds of critical control. Then all we have to do is what we already know we can do: find the creative link between the Exquisite Corpse sentence and our problem.

So here is an example of the Exquisite Corpse technique in action. We need a sentence to help us address the problem of becoming more creative in everything we do.

We start by randomly generating the words that form our Exquisite Corpse sentence. Let's assume our team members come up with the following words:

Adjective: The peculiar
Noun: Bicycle
Verb: Swims
Adjective: A brilliant
Noun: Banana

So our Exquisite Corpse sentence becomes *"The peculiar bicycle swims a brilliant banana."* This is Light Bulb #2.

Light Bulb #1:
Our business today

Light Bulb #3:
The ideas we generate to become more creative

Light Bulb #2:
Our stimulus: "The peculiar bicycle swims a brilliant banana"

This is similar to the Random Word method we discussed earlier, only now we have a Random Sentence. To make sure it is indeed random, it is essential that each participant writes down his or her word before hearing anybody else's.

Now we interrogate the sentence and see where it takes us, bearing in mind the problem we are trying to solve. That is, how do we become more creative in everything we do?

Here are just a few thought starters from the sentence.

Peculiar:

How can we apply this word to help us get ideas about becoming more creative? We address the word "peculiar".

- We can ask ourselves, what makes something peculiar? Perhaps something that doesn't fit with our preconceived ideas. A departure from the norm. Strangely interesting. A disconnection. Something beyond the obvious.
- If you use any word too often it begins to lose its meaning or at least its impact. "Creative" can become just another

word. How about if we redefine it as Peculiar? That will
make us take a fresh look at the subject.

- Peculiar makes me think of pecuniary, or finance, which in
  turn leads to returns or value. So what is the value of being
  Creative? What return do you get from being Creative?

- Exploring pecuniary might not actually give us direct ideas
  about becoming more creative, but it could provide help in
  convincing people who are skeptical about creativity. Or
  who are not involved in the decision-making process about
  being more creative, but who will be expected to adopt the
  new Creative ways.

- Think of it like this... What's the return on the effort every
  time you are Creative? Creativity can take more effort, time
  and energy than the old, obvious ways; particularly while
  practicing or learning to be Creative.

- There has to be a benefit for this. So what is it? It's better
  ideas, better results and better ways of doing things.

- People need to understand this across the organisation to
  engender a positive creative culture.

- In a corporate culture that allows freedom for Creativity,
  people speak the same language; they interact with each
  other to generate new ideas; they can support and
  understand each other.

Bicycle:

Now, what ideas about creativity can be generated by thinking
about a bicycle?

- A bicycle has no reverse gears. Creativity is not about
  going backwards, it's about going forward.

- Bicycles are maneuverable and flexible, and creativity requires that flexibility too. We have to break down rigid behaviours.

- They say if you learn to ride a bicycle you remember it forever. Perhaps if we teach someone how to be creative, they could be creative forever.

- When you learn to ride, you use training wheels... those little wheels at the back that stop the bicycle from tipping over. We could help our budding creative people by providing "training wheels" for them. That is, we could teach them the skills and then give them a safe environment where they can practice their new skills. Take away the fear of falling by helping them, supporting them, encouraging them. Give them small tasks at first to practice on and don't expect them to solve the company's biggest problems.

- To encourage us to ride, the bicycle seat is comfortable. But if you sit back and pedal comfortably you won't ride very fast. To ride faster, you stand up and you push yourself. Similarly, to promote creativity you need a certain amount of comfort. But if our people become too comfortable they won't be stimulated to greater creativity. If we want to push creativity further, like the bicycle, we have to give up some comfort. Standing up and pedaling is like adding some pressure, some competition, or perhaps, a deadline.

- Some bicycles have passenger seats. If someone is sitting there in the passenger's seat and you are doing all the pedaling it can hold you back. Like if some people are "passengers" in adopting the new creative ways. We have to identify the passengers and get them to pedal with us.

- However if the two of you are on a tandem bicycle which has two sets of pedals, you can make tremendous progress working (pedaling) together towards a more creative organisation.

- Bicycles have bells that signal others in order to avoid accidents. Or to say "hi" to someone you know or would like to know. This thinking can make us take notice of other people's views about being creative and to learn from them. Or to warn others that you have adopted a new creative approach so they are not overwhelmed when confronted by your new ways.

- As for saying "hi", you should stay alert to meeting new people who might share your views on creativity or to offer their views about being more creative.

Swims:

How can the word "swims" help us get ideas about becoming more creative?

- Swimming. Floating. Float on the surface. It's like creativity. Don't go too deep, too fast - float across the surface.

- Let everyone float their ideas. Don't criticise ideas. Don't sink unusual ones. Give everything a chance to float. Encourage floating.

- There are many swimming strokes for different occasions. Get lots of ideas before going into any of them deeply. How can we do this? Set up protocols for how we all react to each others' ideas. Ban negative words and phrases. Schedule time for reflection in-between idea generation and evaluation.

- People wear goggles when swimming to allow them to see things more clearly. Put on metaphorical goggles when looking at other people's creative efforts. Learn from their ideas and experiences.
- And just as you improve your swimming with practice, the more you try being creative the better you get at it.

Brilliant:

Again, we use this word to help us focus on becoming more creative. What ideas can we get?

- There are two meanings to brilliant:
  - Brilliant as in clever. Yes we want that. Clever ideas are ones that work. Creativity must also 'work' for us. It must be practical, not just peculiar.
  - The second meaning to brilliant might be shiny, colourful and bright. That's what creativity is. Something that stands out like a flash of brilliance. Something colourful in an otherwise drab world. Like a butterfly.
- Butterflies in the stomach. The awkward feeling you get when you're nervous. When something is creative, the creator is always nervous. She can't prove it will work. She believes it will, but she's apprehensive.
- So does the opposite apply? If it doesn't make me nervous, it's not creative? Probably. So we should add butterflies to everything we do. If it doesn't give me butterflies in the stomach, it's not creative enough. Go back... do it again.
- We could use the butterfly to merchandise this idea. *Add Butterflies*. Let's put it into our language. Let's use pictures of butterflies to remind us what we must do. Let's ask of

each other's ideas... "Does it give you butterflies?" If not, then *"add butterflies"*.

Finally, we can get ideas about creativity by interrogating the word "banana".

- A banana is a source of energy. Creativity needs energy. Have we an energetic environment? What is stopping us from being energetic? Are some procedures sapping energy? Is the temperature right? Not comfortably warm, but comfortably cool. What can we do to push up the energy levels?
- Bananas are yellow. Yellow is sometimes said to represent fear. And fear stifles creativity. What can we do to reduce fear amongst our people? How can we help them overcome the fear of rejection, failure, ridicule? To encourage creativity we have to reward it. Even if a creative idea isn't put into practice, the generator of that idea must be rewarded; so long as the idea is both practical and peculiar.
- Bananas need to be peeled. How can we peel away all the creativity "stoppers". Peel back the layers of hierarchy and formality. Create an environment free from the rules that limit the creative process.
- Bananas get bruised easily when not properly cared for. People can also get bruised if their views on creativity are not handled with care and sensitivity, or if they are not supported while they are becoming more creative themselves.
- Bananas... Pajamas. Pajamas make us think of going to bed. Putting tired ideas and old ways of thinking to bed.

All that and more from a seemingly silly sentence. You can imagine just how many wonderful ideas you could generate by applying four or five heterogeneous minds in this manner.

Now that we've been through this example, I can tell you that this is a real business case. Early in 2002 I met with the senior members of one of the world's most prominent advertising agencies and we addressed this very topic using the Exquisite Corpse tool.

Tips On Using Exquisite Corpse

- You need five or more people
- You need time to explore the topic thoroughly: a minimum of one hour.
- Every participant needs to believe in the method.
- You need five random words: an adjective, a noun, a verb, an adjective, a noun.
- Choose positive adjectives rather than negative ones. They help you envisage a better future.
- Choose tangible nouns. They help you visualise.
- Choose unusual words. Get creative with it.
- Make sure the words are decided upon before you share them. You don't want anyone to be influenced by someone else's word.
- Let your minds go. Get behind the words. For example, think about their features and benefits. Explore.
- Be positive, not critical of the ideas that spring forth.
- Write down everything that is suggested.
- Review the ideas at a separate session.

Topics For Exquisite Corpse

You can use this method to address any qualitative issue. But try reserving it for more complex problems and use the more straightforward tools for easier ones. Here are some sample questions:

1. How can we improve our customer service?
2. How can we structure our company more efficiently?
3. How can we attract better people to our business?
4. What new product ideas can we develop?
5. How can we differentiate our brand from the competition?
6. How can we present our business credentials in a more creative way?

While Exquisite Corpse is of most value when used by a team, you might like to try it by yourself. If so, choose from one of the sentences used by others. Without reading them first, pick a number between 1 and 10, then that will be your Exquisite Corpse sentence. Alternatively you can go to www.creativeswitch.com and generate your own.

1. The plastic house talks a wonderful potato.
2. A succulent starburst creates beautiful success.
3. A carpeted mirror sweeps an unusual newspaper.
4. An amazing sock pounces (on) a vigilant hand-phone.
5. A fat handle shouts (at) an excited jelly.
6. A shrewd pumpkin surfs a shiny bus.
7. A delicious pencil opens a crazy letterbox.

8. The metal parachute jumps (over) an up-side-down clock.
9. A sexy refrigerator tightens a thoughtful cheese.
10. A surprising suitcase kisses a wide screwdriver.

Now having chosen your sentence, don't be tempted to trade it for another that looks easier or more interesting or closer to your problem.

Let your mind go. See where the sentence leads you. Just be careful not to find ways to link your sentence to ideas you already have. And don't settle for the early ideas. Push yourself to go further and find the less obvious ones.

Some Exquisite Exercises

1. Why do you think the following sentence might be a poor stimulus for business problem?

   An efficient businessman walks a nice computer.

2. Think of 10 unusual adjectives. Make them vivid ones.

3. Visualize the following. (It helps to close your eyes – but not when you're reading them!)
   - Excruciating picture-frame
   - Liquid Lamborghini
   - Sharpened pram
   - Singing licorice-vases
   - Hairy windscreen-viper

4. Which word from each of these pairs is more thought provoking and why?

jelly bean	candy
flamboyant	colorful
cat	tiger
chair	chaise lounge
incredulous	unbelievable
kaleidoscope	telescope

12
Get the Creative Habit

A: One.

Q: How many psychics does it take to change a light bulb?

We spoke earlier about the Creative Habit (Chapter 5). We said that it is like any other habit in that it can be learned, practiced, mastered, done often and done easily. Of course, to get the Creative Habit we need to understand Creativity and how it works. Let's do a quick revision.

1. Creativity, we said, can be defined as the merging of ideas which have not been merged before. New ideas are formed by developing current ones within our minds. We used the Light Bulbs as our graphic reminder and we learned how to force connections between two seemingly unrelated things.

2. Creativity is essential in today's competitive world. It brings an ROI to individuals, companies and countries. The second ROI, Relevance, Originality and Impact, are the measures of creativity itself. You need all three.

3. We can all be creative, although sometimes our preconditioning prevents us. But we are what we EAT and if we set the creative Environment, get the creative Attitude and learn the creative Tools all of us can be more creative.

4. Creativity comes easier when we learn to connect things in our heads. The more there is in there, the more connections we can make. We called it Exponential Creative Potential and noted that it comes through increased knowledge and experience.

5. We discussed how much of what we do is given over to habit and how our old habits may not be applicable in today's world.

6. And then we looked at six Creative Tools that will help us attack our problems and opportunities in more creative ways. The Tools act as second Light Bulbs and provide the stimulus to more creative solutions.

You now have everything you need to *flick your creative switch*. But to help you on your way, here are a few more tips.

Which Tool for Which Task?

You may have already formed some opinions about which tools you like and which ones you don't. Let me encourage you to put aside your bias for now and to try all of them a couple of times before deciding which are for you, because there might be a place for all of them in your Creative Thinking repertoire.

All the tools can be used to help you think creatively about any sort of challenge you face, however some tools are more suited to certain tasks than others. There is a handy table included on the next page to help you decide when to use each tool.

Still can't decide which tool? Try this creative approach… Give each tool a number from one to six and roll a die. Or better still, make your own die with one tool on each side. Then roll away. (Lucky I didn't show you seven tools.)

Don't Rush It

Earlier we spoke about necessity being the mother of invention. Well, there's another saying about mothers. This one comes from Brazil: "Haste is the mother of imperfection". If you really want great results from these tools, don't rush them. Give them time to work. And give yourself time to master them. It will pay off.

	Curly Questions	Eyes of Experts	What's Hot?	Random Word	Extremes	Exquisite Corpse
By yourself	✦	✦	✦	✦	✦	
Small team (2-4 people)	✦	✦	✦	✦	✦	
Larger team (5-10 people)	✦			✦		✦
Advertising/Promotions			✦	✦	✦	
Strategic decisions	✦	✦				✦
Personal issues	✦	✦		✦		
Staffing issues	✦	✦				✦

60 Ways to Build Your Creative Habit

All of these ideas are ways to get you to break with tradition, to build your knowledge or experiences or to force new connections. Try them.

1. Listen to an unfamiliar radio station. Perhaps talkback radio. You'll discover what the average person thinks is important.
2. Watch a TV program you know you won't like. You might be wrong.

3. Have a wrong hand day. Do everything with your opposite hand and force your brain to work in a different way.
4. Persevere with a cryptic crossword puzzle. Learn the little tricks and see what an interesting challenge cryptic crosswords can be.
5. Even if you can't draw well, try drawing familiar things in unfamiliar ways. For example, how an ant would see a man. When you do this you get a different perspective of everyday things. You will also be less inclined to expect your drawings to be photographically accurate.
6. Get off the train one stop early and walk home down some different streets and find something new.
7. Read a book you've had on your bookshelf but have never read.
8. Open a familiar book at random and read one page. Force yourself to find one new word or idea there that you can use tomorrow.
9. Look through your wardrobe and find an unfamiliar combination of clothes to wear.
10. Sign off your letters and emails in a different way. (My colleague James Glenn always signs off with "Be sen-say-tional!")
11. Give every idea a chance to succeed. Instead of automatically rejecting ideas that sound like they won't work, give the idea a chance. Ask yourself, "How can I make this work?" If after examining the idea you can't make it work, then reject it. But by giving every idea a chance to succeed you'll find many possible or partial solutions you would have otherwise rejected. (Now don't say this idea won't work!)

12. Watch a cartoon on TV and find similarities between the plot and what is happening in your personal life.

13. Examine how you do things. Ask yourself questions, like: Why do we always do it this way? Is there a better way to do this?

14. Remove yourself from your usual workspace and go somewhere else to think through a problem. Maybe a coffee shop or a park. A change of scenery may spark a different way of thinking.

15. Reorganize your office space. Add visual or aural stimuli.

16. Stare at a piece of abstract art and find 10 possible meanings to it.

17. Visit websites that contain brain teasers and try the puzzles. Just go to your search engine and type in "brain teasers" or "mind games".

18. Have an unbirthday. Make tomorrow your unbirthday and treat yourself to what you want to do. Make it something unusual.

19. Write a story called "My Perfect Day of Work". Don't think much about it... just start writing and use your imagination to create your perfect day. Then you'll know what you really want and you can start making it happen.

20. Keep a note book and pen by your bed and when you wake up, write down everything you remember about your dreams. Then force yourself to find some meaning in the dreams.

21. Read a children's book and find some relevant meaning to a problem or an opportunity you face.

22. Try working at a colleague's desk for a change. You'll get a new view.

23. Attempt a household chore or negotiate your office with your eyes closed. This will force you to use other senses.
24. Don't just take things as they seem. Try using a small mirror; literally to look at things differently.
25. Break with adult inhibitions. For example, read out loud to yourself.
26. Try singing the words of a problem you are trying to solve. Maybe put them into a chant.
27. Sit underneath your desk to see the office differently.
28. Find a really noisy place and try to shut out the din with your thoughts.
29. Give your taste buds a surprise. Try ordering the item you like **least** on a fast-food menu.
30. If you normally sit down to think, stand up.
31. Set your alarm for 3am. Write down whatever comes into your head when you wake up. Write one full page. In the morning, force yourself to find significant meaning in what you've written.
32. If you normally drive, sit in one of the back seats for a while. (But don't try driving from that position.)
33. Get on the first bus that you see. Go to the end of the line and discover what's there.
34. Improve your motor skills. Juggle tennis balls. (Don't try knives until you master 17 tennis balls.)
35. Wear odd socks for a day and see how many people notice. Also notice how less self-conscious about it you become during the day.
36. Write notes with your wrong hand. (Who knows. They might be easier to read than your normal handwriting.)

37. Find images in abstract patterns on marble or wallpaper. This gives you something to do when you're just sitting you-know-where.
38. Create a meal using ingredients beginning with the letter "C". Or "D".
39. Be the first to say "hello" to everyone you meet.
40. Memorise five towns in Croatia for no other reason than making your brain work harder.
41. Eat toast butter-side-down and see if it tastes different.
42. Photograph your five favourite buildings in your city. Figure out why they are your favourites.
43. Sketch your partner in pencil. Hint: don't show it if it makes her look fatter. Or him look balder.
44. Make up your own words. Start with a word for a taxi driver with an empty cab who drives straight past you while you wave frantically. Make it original and keep it clean.
45. Find new meanings in common words by reading them backwards.
46. Set your watch 5 hours 10 minutes forwards and stay punctual.
47. Have a lengthy conversation with a child.
48. Make up phrases by treating the letters on car number plates as acronyms.
49. Find a really ugly painting and force yourself to see beauty in it.
50. Listen to a foreign language radio station.
51. Learn to say hello in 20 languages.
52. Donate extravagantly to a beggar.
53. Walk backwards at home.

54. Read a magazine on a completely new subject.
55. Get lost in your home town.
56. Learn a really interesting phrase in Swahili. Use it in conversation.
57. Work out your salary per second in your head. (Are you worth it?)
58. Drive 10% slower than normal. See how much longer it takes to get there.
59. Use food colouring to make a blue omelet. Eat it.
60. Do absolutely nothing for seven minutes.

Flick Your Creative Switch

So now you know how to *flick your creative switch* and get the Creative Habit. Remember, the Creative Habit is like any other habit in that it becomes stronger with use. So practice using these creative tools and look for other opportunities to *flick the switch*.

Let's take one last look at the three Light Bulbs.

Think of Light Bulb #1 as you and how you do things now. Think of Light Bulb #2 as everything we've been discussing in this book. Now, *flick your creative switch*. As you go about your professional and personal life, force the two together and see how much more creative you can become.

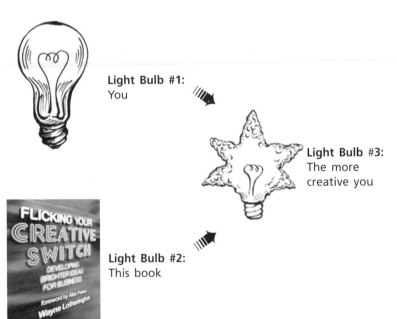

Light Bulb #1:
You

Light Bulb #3:
The more
creative you

Light Bulb #2:
This book

Stay in Touch

I hope you've enjoyed *Flicking Your Creative Switch.* If you have any comments or creative ideas you'd like to share, I'd be delighted to hear from you. If you use these tools and you get the results you're looking for, email me and tell me what you've done. Or if you're having problems making them work, let me know and I'll see if I can help.

Send your emails to wayne@allsorts.com.sg

Or visit our website: www.creativeswitch.com

Now work on that Creative Habit!

Solutions

Page 14
Gottschaldt figurine
This is where the phrase comes
from: *thinking out of the box.*

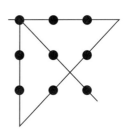

This is a lateral thinking answer.

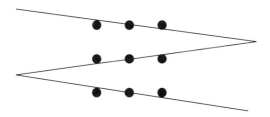

Pages 16 and 17
Easy when you know how!

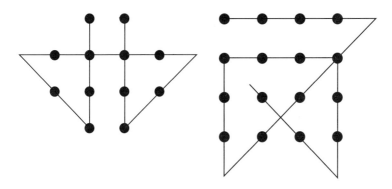

Pages 100 and 101
1D, 2F, 3H, 4A, 5G, 6E, 7C, 8J, 9B, 10I.

References

Ades, Dawn. *Surrealist Art*. Chicago: Thames and Hudson, 1997.

Bryan, Mark, et al. *The Artists Way At Work: Riding the Dagron*. New York: Quill, 1999.

Butler, E and Madsen, P. *Boost Your IQ*. London: Pan Books, 1990.

Buzan, Tony. *Make the Most of Your Mind*. London: Colt Books, 1988.

Conrad, Michael. *Reach for the Stars: Best Bar None*. Chicago: Leo Burnett, 1999.

Covey, Stephen R. *The 7 Habits of Highly Effective People*. London Pocket Books, *1999*

De Bono, Edward. *The Mechanism of the Mind*: Intl Ctr for Creative Thinking, 1992.

De Bono, Edward. *Seriously Creative*. London. Harper Collins, 1996

De Bono, Edward. *Six Thinking Hats*. Little Brown & Co, 1990.

Gamez, George. *Creativity: How to Catch Lightning in a Bottle*. Los Angeles: Peak Publications, 1996.

Innovation House. *Innovation House tutorial on creativity, brainstorming and innovation*. URL: http://www.infinn.com/innovationhouse.html 2001

James, William. http://www.emory.edu/EDUCATION/mfp/james.html

Kroehnert, Gary. *100 Training Games*. Sydney: McGraw-Hill, 1996.

Kroehnert, Gary. *Taming Time*. Sydney: McGraw-Hill, 1999.

Levenson, Bob. *Bill Bernbach's Book*. New York: Villard Books, 1987.

Light Bulb Jokes. http://www.lightbulbjokes.com/directory/p.html

Love, John F. *McDonald's: Behind the Arches.* Great Britain: Bantam Books, 1989.

MacKenzie, Gordon. *Orbiting the Giant Hairball.* New York: Viking, 1996.

McAlhone, Beryl & Stuart, David. *A Smile in the Mind.* London: Phaidon Press, 2001.

Michalko, Michael. *Cracking Creativity.* Berkeley: Ten Speed Press, 1998.

Mukerjea, Dilip. *Surfing the Intellect.* Singapore: The Brainware Press, 2001

Mukerjea, Dilip. *Superbrain.* Singapore: Oxford University Press, 1996

Ornstein, Robert. *The Right Mind: Making Sense of the Hemispheres.* New York: Harcourt Brace and Co., 1997.

Ornstein, Robert. *Evolution of Consciousness.* New York: Simon & Schuster, 1992.

Pease, Barbara & Allan. *Why Men Don't Listen & Women Can't Read Maps.* Australia: Pease Training International, 1999.

Reinhard, Keith. *Bill Bernbach Said.* New York: DDB Needham, 1994.

Stain, Lois & Hudson, Gladys. *The Story of Paul J. Meyer.* Florida: Lifetime Books, 1986.

Sutton, Robert I. *Weird Ideas That Work.* New York. The Free Press, 2002.

Vaske, Herman. *Why Are You Creative?* New York: fivedegreesbelowzero Press, 2002.

Von Oech, Roger. *A Whack on the Side of the Head.* New York: Warner Books, 1998.

Whitney, Dick & Giovagnoli, Melissa. *75 Cage Rattling Questions.* New York: McGraw-Hill, 1997.

Workshops and Seminars

Wayne Lotherington and his team at Allsorts Habit Creation conduct workshops all over the world. The workshops are all about creating new and better business habits, with special emphasis on Creativity. Topics include:

Creative Thinking — *The Creative Switch*™
Selling Creative — *The Creative Bridge*
Strategic Thinking — *SOCceR*™
Presentation Skills — *Tell it, Jell It, Sell It* ®
Account Management Essentials — *Superheroes*
Time Management — *Time Out*
Personal Motivation — *Achiever*
New Client/Agency Relationships — *Pre-Nup*
Healing Client/Agency Relationships — *ER (Emergency Room)*
Negotiation Skills — *The Road to Negotiation*
Performance Management — *Improving Performance*
Advertising Agency Finance — *Show Me The Money!*
Leadership — *Take Me To Your Leader*
Train the Trainer — *Developing Deputies*

To learn more about these workshops visit www.allsorts.com.au

® Tell It, Jell It, Sell It is a Registered Trademark of Allsorts
™ SOCceR and Creative Switch are trademarks of Allsorts

Q: How many lawyers does it take to change a light bulb?

A: Whereas the party of the first part, also known as "Lawyer," and the party of the second part, also known as "Light Bulb," do hereby and forthwith agree to a transaction wherein the party of the second part (Light Bulb) shall be removed from the current position as a result of failure to perform previously agreed upon duties, i.e. the lighting, elucidation, and otherwise illumination of the area ranging from the front (north) door, through the entryway, terminating at an area just inside the primary living area, demarcated by the beginning of the carpet, any spillover illumination being at the option of the party of the second part (Light Bulb) and not required by the aforementioned agreement between the parties.

The aforementioned removal transaction shall include, but not be limited to, the following steps:

The party of the first part (Lawyer) shall, with or without elevation at his option, by means of a chair, stepstool, ladder or any other means of elevation, grasp the party of the second part (Light Bulb) and rotate the party of the second part (Light Bulb) in a counter-clockwise direction, this point being non-negotiable.

Upon reaching a point where the party of the second part (Light Bulb) becomes separated from the party of the third part ("Receptacle"), the party of the first part (Lawyer) shall have the option of disposing of the party of the second part (Light Bulb) in a manner consistent with all applicable state, local and federal statutes.

Once separation and disposal have been achieved, the party of the first part (Lawyer) shall have the option of beginning installation of the party of the fourth part ("New Light Bulb"). This installation shall occur in a manner consistent with the reverse of the procedures described in step one of this self-same document, being careful to note that the rotation should occur in a clockwise direction, this point also being non-negotiable.

Note: The above described steps may be performed, at the option of the party of the first part (Lawyer), by any or all persons authorized by him, the objective being to produce the most possible revenue for the party of the fifth part, also known as "Partnership."

Index